ALSO BY MARY GORDON

FICTION

NONFICTION

MARY GORDON

SEEING THROUGH PLACES

*Reflections on
Geography and Identity*

A TOUCHSTONE BOOK
PUBLISHED BY SIMON & SCHUSTER
New York London Toronto Sydney Singapore

To my Cousin Peppy,
with whom I have seen many of these places.

TOUCHSTONE
Rockefeller Center
1230 Avenue of the Americas
New York, NY 10020

For information about special discounts for bulk purchases,
please contact Simon & Schuster Special Sales:
1-800-456-6798 or business@simonandschuster.com

Designed by Brooke Zimmer
Text set in Bembo
Manufactured in the United States of America

1 3 5 7 9 10 8 6 4 2

The Library of Congress has cataloged the Scribner edition as follows:

Gordon, Mary, date
Seeing through places: reflections on geography and
identity/Mary Gordon
p. cm.
1. Gordon, Mary, date. 2. Gordon, Mary, date—Childhood and
youth. 3. Women novelists, American—20th century—
Biography. 4. Women novelists, American—20th century—
Family relationships. I. Title.
PS3557.0669Z465   2000
813'.54—dc21   99-22208
[B]   CIP

ISBN 0-684-86254-9
0-684-86255-7 (Pbk)

CONTENTS

MY
GRANDMOTHER'S
HOUSE

SOME DAYS I would be left at my grandmother's house. I never knew why. Usually, I could ask my father anything, but I couldn't ask him that, why I was being left at my grandmother's, because I knew it was a privilege to be in that house, and no one, even my father would understand my reluctance. It was only a partial reluctance anyway, and I believed then that I had no business communicating anything I only partially understood.

Entering the house, I was plunged into an atmosphere of bafflement. The words, the manners, all the things, were foreign to me. The foreignness almost seemed literal; often I didn't understand what the people in my grandmother's house were saying, and often what I said was not understood.

What do I mean by understand? There were names for things that I found unfamiliar: "commode" for toilet, "box" for the area of the floor where the dog was made to lie, "pantry" for a series of shelves on one of the kitchen walls. My mother used these words easily, but she didn't use them to describe anything in our house. Or our apartment, what my father and I called home but what was to her something else. Something serious and untemporary. Something that generated no names proper to itself. In her mother's house, my mother knew that everything had been named long ago, once and for all.

I had trouble placing my grandmother's house. I knew it had nothing to do with America. Or postwar life. And yet it stood at the center of the lives of all her children and her children's children. It expressed an era—historical, perhaps, wholly imaginary, that we grandchildren only vaguely understood. We knew that it had ended long before we were born; it seemed to have touched upon our parents' early childhood, but we weren't sure. There were twenty-one grandchildren who visited my grandmother's house regularly. Of her nine children, only two had settled more than ten miles away from her. We all lived on Long Island, in towns that bordered Queens and took their identity more from "the city" than "the island." My grandmother had lived in the same house since 1920, when the area was farmland; she despised the people who had moved there from Brooklyn or the Bronx after the war. She condemned new houses and the objects in them.

Each object in her house belonged to the Old World. Nothing was easy; everything required maintenance of a complicated and specialized sort. Nothing was disposable, replaceable. There were no errors of taste because there were no imaginable other choices. I was not unhappy there; each object's rightness of placement made me feel honored to be among them. Yet I was always guilty among those things, as if they knew I preferred what was in my glamorous aunt's house. She lived in the next town from my grandmother's; her husband owned a liquor store and made more money than anyone we knew. My aunt and uncle bought things easily, unlike the rest of the family, and so the house was full of new or newish objects: the plastic holders for playing cards, like shells or fans, the nut dishes in the shape of peanuts, the corn dishes in the shape of ears of corn, the hair dryer like a rocket, the makeup mirror framed by lightbulbs, the bottles of nail polish, the ice bucket, the cocktail shaker, the deep freeze. And the house was stocked with pleasurable things to eat, drink, sit on, listen to, lean against, watch, sleep in, ride, or wear. I knew these pleasures to be inferior, but I sank into them each time, stealing their luxury and fearing for my soul, as I half feared for my aunt's which I couldn't imagine to be the same, interested as she was in having a good time.

My grandmother had no interest in having a good time—that is, in doing anything that would result only in pleasure—and her house proclaimed this, as it proclaimed everything about her. Her house was her body, and like her body, was honorable, daunting, reassuring, defended, castigating, harsh, embellished, dark. I can't imagine how she lived, that is to say how she didn't die of the endless labor her life entailed. Nine children. It's easy either to romanticize her or utterly to push her aside.

Although I wasn't happy there, I did, somehow, like her house. Her garden had old-fashioned flowers, bright colored, a little wild; marigold, cosmos, foxglove, phlox. Older varieties of roses, whose petals seemed thinner than those of more recent types, more susceptible, as my soft flesh was more susceptible than those of the adults around me, to insect bites that made it horrible to the eye. I liked her garden even better than my aunt's, where the greens were deeper than the greens of any leaves or grass I'd seen anywhere else. I linked dark greenness to prosperity, as if my uncle had invested in that greenness so that we would all be more secure. My grandmother's house had no connection to prosperity; it had righteousness instead.

There were three ways you could enter the house: through the front porch, the side porch, or the kitchen. The kitchen was the most common way. Tacked on, it hadn't originally been part of the house. It floated on nothing, it had no foundations, it was a ship that sailed on air. And yet it was a serious place. Difficult and steady work went on there; the kitchen was productive, rigorous. And yet so light! Its lightness was a particular pleasure in summer. The screen door opened with a leisurely, indulgent creak. It bent back on a steel hasp, and even a child could hook it open easily. All the things that kitchen contained: marjoram, nutmeg, green peppercorns, sage from the garden, mason jars of preserved fruit! Some hints of the Italian from my Italian grandfather: ricotta mixed with cinnamon and sugar, almond biscotti, fresh figs purple at the top, fading to a tender green. Irish soda bread my grandmother had learned to make as a girl at home. Inexplicably, hamantaschen—a way of using up the jars and jars of preserved figs. She would save a little dough, a little bit of fig, for me to make my own. She'd put mine in the oven along with hers, but mine were much, much smaller and they always burned. Beside her rows of golden pastry hats were my two burnt offerings, charred and solid black. I would eat them anyway, pretending they were good. I felt I had to, out of loyalty. "Don't eat those things, eat one of my nice ones here," she'd always say, and, guiltily, I would.

What was this all about? She was an expert baker. Why didn't she put my pastries in first and take them out before she put hers in? Or put mine in later, so they'd be ready at the same time as hers? What was she trying to show me? That I could try and try but would never be as good as she? That I should not have trusted her? That I should always keep an eye out, because whatever I did in life would be my own affair? It never occurred to me that the situation could be any different. My grandmother's implacable posture made the idea of alternatives impossible. What was, was. Because it had to be.

That kitchen was a monument to her refusal to accept the modern world. The sink was deep and had two narrow spigots, made of brass, that let out only thin, slow streams of water, unlike the jubilant spurts from the stainless steel faucets of ordinary fifties sinks. The table was white deal, with a seam down the middle where it could be made to fold, but it was never folded. My grandmother would run a knife blade through that seam and the ones along the sides, to dislodge crumbs of dried food. This was the sort of thing she was doing when people perceived her as being still. The linoleum was dull gray with spattered dots of red, yellow, and black. Her dishes were white with gentle floral patterns, pink and blue. I don't know where they might have come from.

There were a lot of things around the house that, like those dishes, suggested a half-glimpsed gentility. If you went into the side porch, for example, which you rarely did, there were objects of mimed opulence: black jardinieres with Oriental scenes painted on them, holding palms or tall, full philodendrons. The side porch had been my grandfather's workroom; he'd been a jeweler. He died when I was one year old. The room was kept purposely useless, in memory of him. I often stayed there, lonely, feeling I'd stolen grace.

In my grandmother's house I was often alone, left to myself because my grandmother was always busy. Sometimes she'd include me in her tasks: I would hold open the trapdoor so she could carry the wash up from the basement. She'd ask me to hold the funnel steady so she could pour antifreeze into the car. Sometimes I'd help her find a thimble or a pin while she was sewing at her machine; her thick foot in its black, low-heeled oxford pushing her treadle. The words she spoke when at her sewing machine seemed ancient to me, and she was the only one I'd ever heard using them: "rickrack," "grosgrain," "dotted swiss." Nothing she sewed was for me, nothing was for anyone I knew. I never understood what happened to all that sewing; it disappeared magically like sewing for the dead, her black foot steady on the treadle like the hoof of fate.

She rarely talked. She lifted pots and tools and basketfuls of earth and bowls of vegetables. She tore meat off bones and carcasses and made it into soup; she beat eggs into silky custards. I believe she very much enjoyed her life. But she had no time to play with children. And so I wandered the dark house alone, from room to room, beginning with the dark porch, where my bachelor uncle, who still lived with her, slept, winter and summer. There was a piano on the porch, and bound music books nobody opened, full of songs no one I knew had ever sung. "Believe Me, If All Those Endearing Young Charms," "Columbia, the Gem of the Ocean," "High Above Cayuga's Waters," "Eli Yale!" And odd pieces of sheet music, "My Buddy," "I'll Take You Home Again, Kathleen."

Why did they make my uncle sleep there? It was cold in winter, hot in summer. He slept on a couch that was only the semblance of a bed, camouflaged each morning with a gray-and-red-spotted cover. There was almost no place for his things; I don't know where he put his clothes. But I have no understanding of how my uncle lived. I've never come across anybody like him, anyone who would even give me a clue to why he was the way he was. He conformed to no type.

He served the family, especially his mother, with the devotion of a pilgrim to a sacred shrine. He surprised them all by marrying at forty-three—one of the happiest marriages I have known, but that was later. Throughout his twenties and thirties, the family thought of him as at their beck and call. He was a strong, handsome man, a champion athlete, head at one time of all the lifeguards on Jones Beach. Yet they expected him to do their bidding, to be at their service when they needed him. There were nine brothers and sisters; all but two of them had mates or children. Someone was always sick or weak or broke or down on his luck. They called and he arrived.

Just this year, seven years after his death at seventy-four, his wife told me that he had decided when he was fourteen that he would dedicate his life to making his mother's life easier. He made the decision when he saw her fixing the roof during a storm. She was six months pregnant, nailing down tarpaper while the wind blew and the rain fell in torrents. He told her to go inside, that he'd take care of everything. From that time on, for nearly thirty years, that was his job: taking care of everything. When he married, it was his only defiance of my grand-mother. She fainted at the wedding, which wasn't a Mass: he was marrying a non-Catholic. He moved seven miles away. He moved his things off the porch, his few things with their male smells: *Popular Mechanic* magazines, tur-pentine, neat's-foot oil. Things I always stood far away from if I ever wandered onto his part of the porch, avert-ing my eyes and fixing them on the garlands, green and pink, around the words of the sheet music on the piano— "I'll Take You Home Again, Kathleen."

★   ★   ★

One of my mother's younger sisters, the only one who hadn't married, had taken over the upstairs of the house. The upstairs didn't seem quite connected to the rest, but, unlike the innocent detachment of the kitchen, this disconnection seemed sinister. There was an awkward step down after you reached the top of the staircase leading from the living room. After you stepped down, there were two rooms on the right side of the corridor; a full bathroom (the only one in the house) was on the left. In this bathroom, there was blue-black linoleum on the floor, an old bathtub with claw feet, a small sink, a white wooden bureau, a white wooden washstand, a basin and pitcher, from which protruded overripe philodendron. I had a vague but powerful distaste for what I imagined the water in the pitcher might be like: the slimy stems in the unclear yellow liquid. The old-fashionedness of the bathroom made me feel it wasn't quite hygienic, not like the sky blue tiles, the chrome fittings of my glamorous aunt's bathroom, or the light apple green of the bathroom in our apartment. Only my aunt who lived upstairs used the bathroom regularly; my grandmother used the "commode" in her bedroom downstairs. She emptied it sometime, no one knew when, in the upstairs toilet.

My aunt's bedroom was large, industrial, and cold. There was gray linoleum on the floor; her bed and dresser were gray deal. The walls and trim were painted the same shade of gray. Only a small flowered mat lay on the floor by her bed. Each footfall, even your own, sounded ominous in your ears.

My aunt kept some small boxes of jewelry on her

oversize dresser. I remember one pin: a cluster of false-looking purple grapes. She had many more dresses in her closet than my mother, but none of them had the cool freshness of my mother's summer cottons or the urbane, theatrical fragrance of her winter suits. My aunt didn't keep a bottle of perfume on her dresser like that vessel of transparent amber I so loved to approach among my mother's things.

All these lacks on my aunt's part made me pity her. I felt she'd missed the point of it all: adulthood, womanhood. She'd thrown away her chance, and that seemed connected to her childlessness, her cruelty, her bitter tongue, the dark circles below her eyes, the deep imprint of her vaccination scar, her miserliness, her law-abidingness, the way she would dream aloud about the new appliances and modern furniture she'd seen on TV. I pitied her and yet I feared her; no one else could make me feel so bad. My wrongs were so abundant: talking too much, not being quick enough to help clear the table, reading too much, dreaming, dreaming. Her hair was thick and black; her eyes light brown and surveillant. She was thought a beauty; I could not understand why.

The room next to my aunt's was another place in the house, like the front porch, that I couldn't comprehend. It had four iron cots and a gray iron bunk bed. It was nearly always empty. When I asked why my uncle couldn't use that room instead of sleeping on the porch, or half the porch, my mother said, "It has to be like that. In case people need to stay over." But who needed to stay over? Everyone in the family had less than half an hour's drive to get to my grandmother's house. Twice a year, perhaps, the two families who lived far away—in Baltimore, in Philadelphia—might or might not arrive. Meanwhile, my uncle slept outside.

I'd walk around this empty room, set up like a dormitory, remembering that this was where my mother had slept as a child. The oldest, she always had to share a bed with the next youngest baby. I heard all this, but I didn't believe any of it. The child who was my mother, who lived not with me but in this house, was no one I could have known. The girl who slept in this room was not my mother. That girl had died at the moment of my birth. My mother was someone I had given birth to; whatever had gone before had sunk, like a stone in dark water, into the oblivion of life before me. She was dead, the girl my mother was; this empty room with the blank iron beds and the walls that echoed when I shouted out my mother's name, was only a shrine kept for the veneration of the dead.

I didn't like staying upstairs for long, so I'd walk down to the living room, which was a place where no one ordinarily spent time. Both the living room and the dining room, where meals were had only on holidays, were about display. There was a sad, apologistic falseness to them. They were rooms that had to appear to be inhabited; occasional actual habitation was a by-product, a necessary and regretted step that had to be got through to reach the true and desired end: display. The motif of the living room was pastoral. Fragonard's aristocrats gamboled in high-heeled boots and feathered hats on the front faces of the maroon table lamps, curlicued gilt mirrors, inexplicable bibelots: a venetian glass lady's slipper, a floral cup and saucer stood on a shelf beside life-size heads of the Mater Dolorosa and of Jesus suffering beneath the Crown of Thorns. The tears congealed on her cheeks; sweat made bumps on his brow, which I liked to run my fingers over, fearing I'd sinned by taking pleasure in the Savior's represented anguish. It was the texture in itself that captured my attention, not the living memory of the Sorrows of the Lord. On this shelf there was also a thin black stork riding on a turtle's back. I'd been told that it was originally bronze, but I had no reason to believe that. No one ever touched it; it stood for my grandmother's astonishing fecundity, nine children, all born healthy, all still alive. Beside the stork there was a clump of peat, wedge shaped and porous, that she'd brought from Ireland. She arrived in 1897, alone, at seventeen, to be met by strangers and to take up a domestic's life.

There were no pictures in the living room or in the dining room or in the halls or on the stairways or on the front or side porches. The pictures, all religious, were clustered together in my grandmother's small bedroom. Her bedroom on the first floor had no door, only a doorway. Anyone could go inside it at any time; we imagined she could always see out of that room, see whatever we were doing. All her grandchildren made several ostensibly aimless trips into her room each visit. We did it to frighten ourselves. The room was particularly frightening at night.

Her smells: lavender, ammonia, Pine Sol (always at the bottom of the commode), a green pool reminding you inevitably of the corruption that you, as a human being, had no right pretending you could rise above. Old lace, smelling of dust—hair oil, liniment. Unmodern smells that seem to us Indian or pagan, rising from darkness punitive or curing: we could not tell which.

The pictures on her walls were not about pleasing the eye. There was a brown picture with an imprint of Jesus' head: "The Shroud of Turin." Then the words to "Now I Lay Me Down to Sleep" on a blue background, framed with an ivory border. A picture of Christ with long, smooth, girlish hair, pointing to his Sacred Heart, the size and shape of a pimiento or a tongue. Most mysterious: a picture made of slats. You turned your head one way: it was the Scourging at the Pillar. Another turn of the head produced Jesus Crowned with Thorns. If you looked absolutely straight ahead, you saw the Agony in the Garden. I spent hours looking at that picture, frightened, uncomprehending. It was part of my grandmother's hidden supernal path into the mystery of things, a hard road, unforgiving, made of beaten flesh.

The floor of her bedroom was always undependable. I knew you could push the iron bed against the wall and lift a large part of the floor right up if you grabbed hold of an iron ring and pulled. This was the trapdoor to the basement. I was always afraid that I'd walk into her room one day, heedless, dreaming or reading (which I'd been accused of doing far too much), and hurtle down to the dark basement. I didn't think it would mean my death. I

thought my bones would break and then I would be punished by the family. For what they believed was my chief
offense: not paying attention.

How could I tell them how much and with what life-
and-death intensity I paid attention? They wouldn't want
to know, and anyway they'd say I paid attention to the
wrong things, I thought about the wrong things, which is
why I would never be happy and why I would never
prosper. They were just trying to help me to a good and
happy life.

There was some story about a cousin of my mother's
falling through the trapdoor, landing on his head, then sitting up in my grandmother's bed, his head swaddled in
bandages, and being fed soft-boiled eggs and tea. All the
family despised him. I thought about him—his shame, his
fear. Perhaps he read magazines in the bed or looked all
day at the pictures on the walls while his head reeled and
his vision clouded and he fell in and out of fitful sleep,
knowing they were laughing at him behind the kitchen
door.

∞∞∞∞∞∞∞∞∞∞∞∞∞∞∞

We always arrived at my grandmother's house for family
gatherings late, unhelpful, overdressed, but somehow
daunting to the others. Six other households were represented—only the upstairs aunt wasn't living somewhere
else. But except for my glamorous aunt, her generous,
prosperous husband, and her fashionably dressed children—all exceptional because they lived so modernly, so
differently from everything my grandmother stood for—

the rest were minor characters, undistinguished background figures. Nevertheless, each family but ours had some function: the women cooked and served food, the men carried things, moved furniture. We were simply there, representing something they despised: the outside world.

We were coming from where we lived—not a house but the top half of a house; we called it our apartment, liking the urban sound. It was just three blocks away, but traveling there meant some border had to be crossed. The transition made me fretful and fatigued. Often, going to my grandmother's house, I felt physically ill, as if we were making a journey over difficult mountains and had experienced a change of air.

Arriving at my grandmother's house from our apartment was like walking from a movie set onto a stage where some slow-moving, slightly out of date play was in the middle of the second act. Some operetta: men in moustaches, girls in curls, flowers, horses, women with their hands in muffs, women in dresses with elaborate trains. But this makes the atmosphere sound too pleasant, as if the brocade couches and gilt mirrors were the whole of the house. Underneath the floral playfulness of the decor, there was always that implacable judgment emanating from the body of Grandmother. She never had to say a word or do a thing; her daughters with their cruel tongues, her sons with their strong backs, took care of everything.

At these family parties, everything seemed to take too long: the games, the songs, the meals, the stories. There were no wisecracks, no abbreviations, no slang, no smacks. Everything seemed the same unvarying texture: thick and heavy, serious, unchangeable, forbidding. In our apartment, there were bold patches of vividness, alterations of texture, glass and chrome, striped wallpapers, lamps of a color known as bisque, whose bases looked like ice cream. I would touch them with my tongue; they were delicious, carved and polished, cool. Their satin shades, pinkish and smooth as dresses, gave the room an amorous shadowiness when you lit them at dusk.

I don't know where my mother got our furniture. Or if my parents bought it together, an engaged couple, before the wedding. But that's impossible. My father would never have shopped for furniture. He took pride in ignoring his surroundings. To care about things like furniture would have been for him the proof of an inferior nature. To shop for it with his bride-to-be would have made him feel both emasculated and declassed.

So she must, my mother, have gone shopping by herself. To buy the maple bedroom set, the dresser shellacked on top, the lamps, the carpets, the soft chairs. Was she lonely in this, or exhilarated. She was leaving her mother's house for the first time, at the age of thirty-nine. She'd been a major support of both her parents and when my parents left my grandparents' house for their wedding, my grandfather handed her a card which said on it "You will work till the day you die."

My grandfather was partly right: my mother did work hard. She came home from the lawyer's office in her navy blue suit, putting down her leather purse with its built-in compact, changing into a housedress—crisp, printed, fresh colored—and then she cooked for us. She washed our clothes on a washboard. Originally, she'd used the washing machine in her mother's house, but my upstairs aunt insisted she stop. She said the water bill was sky high. Hadn't my mother thought of that?

My mother was overtired, my father was a failure, they fought nearly all the time, and always about money. I would go up to the attic. Upstairs, away from them, I felt free. What had money to do with me, or I with money? I stood beneath the bare beams, in the emptiness, watching the gold light strike the bare wood floor in straight vertical bars. I would sing loudly so I couldn't hear what they were saying. "I won't give you one red cent for carfare." "You ought to have your head examined." I twirled around and around, pretending my skirts were long and billowing. I thought the dust motes traveling down the shafts of light were a blessed substance, like manna. I was privileged to be in proximity to it, but I would never dream of following the light upward to its source, for who has looked upon the face of God and lived?

The attic was meant to be our storage space, but we had nothing to store. My mother had taken nothing from her mother's house, and my father had lived nowhere: in spare rooms of other people's houses, in hotels. I believed that the people who owned the house before us had stored treasures in the attic for years. Their name was Chamberlain. "English," my father said. Meaning "Protestant, nothing to do with us." I associated those bare beams, that clear light, and all that space with Protestants.

Chamberlain—the clean sound, the clipped-off conso-
nants, the relaxed polysyllable. No need to rush or argue
for the Chamberlains. They'd left a beer stein on one of
the attic windowsills—a black background, green figures
in salmon-colored pantaloons and black tricornered hats.
I never touched it. I believed that if I touched it the
Chamberlains would never come back. I longed for them
to come back and give me retroactive permission to
inhabit their attic. Perhaps they would move in there with
me; I could imagine the sun striking their blond hair.
Sometimes I'd look out the window and imagine I could
see them walking up the street. I'd never met them, but I
knew I'd recognize them the moment they appeared.

From the attic, I could hear my father and the radio.
WQXR: the radio station of the *New York Times*. I'd sneak
up on him and see him conducting a phantom orchestra.
My mother listened to radio serials while she ironed. I
remember the name of one of them: "Yours Truly, Johnny
Dollar." In my memories of my mother ironing, it's always
a summer evening. She sips cool drinks, which she leaves
on the end of the ironing board. Her arms are lovely in
her sleeveless dress, buoyant and fragrant, freckled like an
early apple. The iron hisses on the damp fabric, and the
joyous smell of cleanliness enters the air of the living
room. Then there is the sound of gunshots from the radio
and low, conspiratorial, no-nonsense voices.

We didn't have a television. To watch television, we
went either to my grandmother's or to my glamorous
aunt's. My aunt's TV was in the middle of a room they
called the TV room, but my grandmother's was hidden in

a piece of furniture. Perhaps that way she could pretend to herself most of the time that she hadn't capitulated to modern life. She hadn't bought anything *new*.

To get to the TV, you approached a mahogany console. You opened the doors slowly to see the treasure, hidden like pornography: the turquoise screen with its tiny central moon, the size of a fingernail, that appeared when you turned the dial and disappeared after you turned it off.

On Tuesdays, we went to her house to watch Bishop Sheen. Those nights after the moon vanished and the screen filled in its image, what you saw first was an empty chair. His. The bishop's. And then himself, in his beautifully fitted cassock with its purple sash. (We knew it was purple—all bishops had purple sashes—although we saw only black and white.)

We watched as the bishop sat in silence, a few seconds before he spoke. His eyes seemed transparent. They knew everything. They looked into your sinful soul. There was a blackboard on which he drew diagrams and wrote key words. He said that during the station break his guardian angel erased the blackboard. I believed this, and was thrilled by the conjunction of the supernatural and the technological. When the upstairs aunt told me it was just a joke, I wept against my father's jacket.

I have no memory of what the bishop said, but I know I was convinced of its importance. Here was someone talking about the Faith, just as Edward R. Murrow talked about Russia. The Russians wanted to destroy us, Americans, but particularly Catholics. Communists had a diabolical hatred of the Catholic faith. After Bishop Sheen, we would go into the kitchen and kneel for the Rosary. Or my grandmother, my father, and I would kneel. My mother and my aunt, both being crippled, were allowed to sit. After the regular prayers, we said a special prayer for the Conversion of Russia.

When I was seven years old, my father had a heart attack. The next day my mother and I put some clothes in a suitcase, and in a paper shopping bag, plain brown, a doll and two books, *Fifteen Saints for Girls,* and *Pius X, the Farm Boy Who Became Pope.* In that month, when we hoped my father would live, my mother drove straight from work through the Midtown Tunnel, to Bellevue Hospital where my father, in an oxygen tent, did not recover from his first heart attack, but had another and a fatal third. That month I slept beside my grandmother's large, acrid, reassuring body, in the room of the frightening pictures, the lavender and Pine Sol. My mother slept on the living room couch. Why did no one suggest that we sleep upstairs in my mother's childhood room? What was the impulse that had kept that room inviolate, that had forced my uncle to a heatless porch, that placed my mother on a couch rather than a comfortable bed. I will never know, and soon after it was no longer a question because the room became mine and my mother's. After my father died, we moved to my grandmother's house to live all the time. My grandmother's house became my house, although no one suggested I think of it that way. It must have been important to them—my mother's brothers and sisters, I mean—that I not think of it as mine, that it was still theirs much more than mine, although they'd moved out at least twenty years before, and had their own houses with their own children, my cousins.

What a relief it must have been for my mother to exchange the taxing, if initially exhilarating, role of wife for the familiar, comforting, and comfortable role of daughter. My parents' marriage was not happy, and my mother believed that her life in her mother's house had been a series of joyous moments, joyous adventures, meals, loving exchanges, songs around the old piano, ceremonies, and, what must have been to her, the deepest possibilities of repose. I understood how hard my mother worked to keep our life afloat in the apartment. In her mother's house, she would no longer have to do the wash on the washboard. No one could say anything to her about using the washing machine now, as she'd be contributing her share to the water bill. She wouldn't cook her quick, colorful dinners: hamburgers, sliced tomatoes, canned corn. We would eat, seriously, soberly. My grandmother would do the ironing.

Of course, no one asked me what I thought of the move, and perhaps it was right that they should not have. I was seven years old, and I was in shock. The loss of my father had made me see everything as if it were at the end of a tunnel, dim, inaccessible, and almost impossible to interpret. What could I have said that would have done anything but cause me shame in front of these practical people, who were acting, I'd been told and told, for my own good. Could I have said: "I want to be in a place where my father was, in case he might come back." "Your father is dead," they would have said. "It's time to get on with things." And how could I have said they weren't right?

Getting on with things meant turning the room that had been saved for visitors into a room of regular habitation by two, rather than seven, souls. This meant removing the iron bunk beds and, in a concession to our new tenancy, painting the room.

My mother allowed me to choose the color. And this was a wonderful thing for her to do, for it allowed me to enter into a world without words, and words had failed me, failed to explain the enormity of my loss, failed to console, to pierce the darkness. Color did what words could not. I surrounded myself in questions of pure color. From the Dutch Boy paint shop, with the picture of the smiling blond boy with his cap and brush in the window, I was allowed to take home as many paint samples as I liked. These paint samples weren't, of course, really paint, but small pieces of cardboard, perhaps two by three inches, that were the colors of the paint.

First I had to decide what basic color I would choose. Colors, to me, were always people. My favorite color was blue (I was named for the Virgin, and it was her color) but I knew that blue was the favorite color of many people, and so I said my favorite color was orange, which I knew no one liked best. But this sacrifice made me hate orange, and from that day on I've never bought anything orange, except the fruit. I didn't want blue for my bedroom, it was too much like the color of my inner world. I didn't want green; green was efficient and official, committed to getting on with things. Red was dangerous, purple was too old, yellow was a blond. I wanted something entirely unlike my life, but representing what I wanted my life to be. I chose pink.

But I felt, deeply, that some pinks were hateful. I used to cry every time we passed a pink stucco house, on my way to dance class, because I felt the wrongness of the color to the depths of my soul. Pink should not, I knew, suggest candy. It should bring to mind the floral rather than the edible. And yet there was another risk: I didn't want to venture too near the abject orange. Each day, on my way home from school, I would stop in the paint store for one more sample. The salesman was kind; he understood my anguish. I was surrounded by riches; there was somewhere the possibility of exactly the right choice, but also myriad chances for failure. And if I made the wrong choice I was, as my mother kept telling me, stuck with it. At night, I would spread the samples out on the dining room table, where I was meant to be doing my homework. In the end, it came down to two choices: powder pink or apple blossom. Apple blossom was a little darker; perhaps it had a hint of yellow. That was the one I chose.

My choice was wrong. On the walls, nothing suggesting petals lit by the sun appeared. The color was much darker than the sample had suggested. It was sugary rather than papery; it closed in on us, rather than opening us out into the world.

But, as my mother said, I was stuck. My aunt's friend, a

Polish man, did us the favor of painting the room for free. So it took many, many months—from March until late August. All that time, I slept in my grandmother's room and my mother slept on the couch.

When the room was done, we bought a bookcase which the Polish man stained a maple color; the surface was always sticky, and sometimes books stuck to it, leaving behind a layer of paper. I had my own bookshelf, painted white. On top of it I had my statue of the Guardian Angel, and a plastic model of a shoe from Thom McAn, which was the symbol of the gift certificate for a pair of real shoes I'd given my father the Christmas before he died. My mother bought each of us a cardboard chest of drawers; they were floral, blue and pink, and the drawers did not fit properly.

I have no memory of inhabiting that room with my mother. I slept there, read there, must have been sick there, had nightmares, or wept. But I cannot tell you what it was like to spend time in that place, except to say, how odd, there were no curtains on the windows; it was only later, when I took upon myself its decorations, that curtains were put up, and then they were too short, and so, after a few months, I took them down.

Nor do I have much memory of living in my grandmother's house in the state it was before the renovations. I remember one thing only: the labor required to keep it in shape. My weekends were devoted to helping clean the house. There was no joy in it; it was a grim battle against dirt and disorder. No modern products were employed. Ammonia burnt my eyes and hands, Bon Ami cleanser,

shaken from the gold can with the chicken only half out
of its egg, got under my nails. That I would think of asking to play on a weekend was considered unthinkable. I
had no friends anyway, and why should I be left on my
own to read when my mother and my aunt, both crippled
from polio, and my grandmother in her late seventies
"worked their fingers to the bone." I trace to this my
phobic dislike of housework, and the rage that trait has
caused in men, particularly my first husband who said to
me once, "You don't deserve to live in a house." I was
hurt, but I felt he was right. I felt, not unjustly accused,
not ill-described, simply unmasked.

And then there were the renovations. When my grandmother was eighty, my aunt decided to completely reno-
vate the house her mother had lived in for forty years. To
do it without telling her, do it in a month, when she was
in Florida, so that she would come home to find it all
destroyed.

It was my upstairs aunt's idea, and because I have
always associated her with cruelty, I speculate that this,
too, was a cruel act. I believe that if I could pity my aunt
rather than fear and condemn her, it would be the sign
that I had left the things of childhood behind, at least of
moral childhood. Sometimes, almost, I can do it. I think
of the circumstances of *her* childhood. The third child in
the family to be stricken with polio, she alone was sent
away to a school for crippled children, run by French
nuns. It was on the opposite end of Long Island, and she

was separated from her family, who came on Sundays to bring her a picnic lunch. The nuns sounded sadistic. Thinking it important to make the crippled children self-reliant (they were all on scholarship, all the children of the more-or-less poor), they stressed a lack of pity. Self-pity or pity for others. They were obsessed with cleanliness to the point of mania, to the point of tying rags onto the bottom of the crippled children's feet so that as they shuffled on the wooden floors they would keep them perpetually polished. When I think of my aunt in this way, I can forgive her almost anything. It makes sense of her determination to be sure I had a childhood without pleasure.

Was it rage against her mother for sending her away; rage cooled for thirty-five years, that caused my aunt to come up with the plan? They would knock the kitchen, so light, so insubstantial, off the back of the house. They would turn the dining room into a kitchen/dinette. The table where holidays had been celebrated for nearly half a century, where my grandfather had laid his jewels out for customers to choose among, would be put up in the attic, along with the eighteen chairs that matched it. The wall between the living room and the porch would be knocked down to make one large room. The side porch would become a bathroom and a launderette. The washing machine in the basement would be carted away to the junk heap. The trapdoor would be sealed.

For a month, our house was strangely and unusually filled with men. Tony and Frank, the contractor and the foreman, and Steve the electrician and Bill the plumber. Each morning they came with coffee and doughnuts; the Italians sang, the Irish and the Germans were silent. We pretended that the electrician had a secret crush on my aunt, although he never paid her the slightest bit of attention. Each night we slept with fast-beating, excited hearts: worry that the work wouldn't be finished, eagerness to see what it would be like. My aunt consulted no one; only *she* spoke to the contractors, only *she* looked at the blueprints, only *she* ordered the carpets and the new furniture. The old wood floors would be covered with a broadloom pattern that was called instead of pepper and salt, cinnamon and sugar: dots of brown and white. The brocade couch and chairs and the doilies crocheted by my grandmother would be replaced by something called a sectional, its color called, deceptively, gold. There were orange throw pillows and orange drapes. Instead of maroon and gold Fragonard lamps, there were rough white pottery lamps each with an orange stripe. A Danish modern coffee table, in light pine. The cabinets in the new kitchen would be light pine; there were no handles on the doors, and the kitchen table would be light pine, except that it would be covered, always, by an orange print plastic tablecloth. The linoleum was speckled white and gold.

When my aunt and uncle brought my grandmother back from the airport, she got out of the car like a general inspecting a bomb site. She said nothing. She looked around at her missing kitchen, her missing furniture, the missing history of her whole life. She was completely silent. "Say something, Ma," her children kept saying, one after another, sometimes two at once. But she would not. She went into her bedroom, which, except for the trap-door having been sealed, was the same. She lay down and would not join the party. I remember only a sense of shock, and then false gaiety; tunes played at the piano and sung in desperation, as if everything were going to be all right.

It was not all right again. From that day on, my grand-mother grew old. She went on cleaning and cooking, but the charmless modern surfaces she tended gave her no joy. For the first time in her life, she was the victim of minor illnesses. She got colds and sore throats; she sprained her ankle; she took naps in the afternoon. In a year, she was diagnosed with stomach cancer, and in two years she was dead.

But before she died, something almost as shocking as her illness happened. My aunt, who was forty-six, had been keeping company with a man who'd been in love previously with my mother's best friend, who'd died young of a heart attack, and with my other aunt, who was already married. He'd said he could never marry because of his "hypertension." Each Friday at suppertime, he drove up in his truck (he was a plumber) and carried a box with twenty-four bottles of Budweiser beer down the cellar steps, depositing it in the old coal bin, which was empty, except for some broken kitchen chairs. On Fridays he took my aunt to dinner. Then they would come back and sit in front of the couch (the gold sec-tional) and watch TV. He would drink beer after beer.

When he got unsteady, I was sent downstairs to get his beers. One night, when I was eleven and beginning to develop breasts, he looked down the neck of my nightgown. It was the first time it occurred to me that I had anything a man might be interested in looking at; it was a horrifying thought. When I complained to my mother, she said it wasn't our house, we were lucky my grandmother and my aunt were letting us live there and we couldn't "make waves." Once, when I was bringing him a beer, I saw him pinching my aunt's breast. I determined that no man would do that to me, ever.

One Saturday morning, my aunt married him, telling none of us. As it turned out, it was First Saturday and I was at Mass on the way to a school trip to Radio City. I walked into church with my friends to find my aunt on the altar, a bride.

I have never known why she did this, so senselessly, so precipitately, so obviously near to my grandmother's death. Perhaps she couldn't stand to live near the dying one more minute. Or perhaps she was pregnant. It was possible, although unlikely; she was forty-six, she'd never borne a child. I suspect this because I once came upon her going through my closet, stealing sanitary napkins from my box.

My grandmother died. The collapse, the multiple collapses, began. Within six months, her oldest son, the black sheep of the family, was dead of a cancer identical to his mother's. Another aunt developed cancer of the throat.

My mother began drinking. She and my aunt of the secret marriage became enemies. The family split into two camps, my aunt's side and my mother's; because both had been living in my grandmother's house and she had died without a will, both felt the house was theirs.

On the evening of Labor Day, three months after my grandmother's death, we came home from a barbecue to find the living room emptied of furniture, my mother's papers dumped in a heap, like piles of dried dead leaves. My mother's papers, whose order she treasured as a way of showing her mastery over anything official, anything typed or printed on a letterhead, anything that proved she had never been and never would be a penny or a dime in debt, were exposed, shamefully, in the center of the room.

For a year, my aunt and mother struggled. My mother's boss, a lawyer, represented her. My aunt hired a stranger. The argument was this: my mother had paid the mortgage on the house from the beginning of the Depression till she left to marry my father seventeen years later. After she left, the other siblings were required by my aunt to divide the mortgage payment into nine equal parts, one part for each child. This arrangement went on until my grandmother's death. My mother said that my aunt, who had a good salary, had lived rent free for thirty years, whereas she'd contributed a disproportionate amount of her salary to the upkeep of the house in her single years. My aunt countered that she'd bought new furniture, paid for the wall-to-wall carpeting, and had shared equally with my mother in the cost of the renova-tions. In the end, the ownership of the house was given to my mother and my aunt was to be paid what she'd contributed toward the renovation. But the family, that fully leaved tree of so many strong branches that had grown from my grandmother's body, was split in two. There was never again harmony, never a wedding or a graduation without a scene, never a night after the night of the stealing of the furniture when my mother didn't go to sleep stupefied by enough glasses of sweet vermouth to keep her from the painful truth of all that had been lost or stolen from her.

It was not a good thing that my mother got the house, not a good thing for the house, certainly, not a good thing for me, and I think (though I can't be sure, considering the alternatives) that it was not a good thing for my mother. The house was too much for her. Perhaps it would always have been too much for her; one person, handicapped, with a full-time job and a bookish daughter who couldn't be counted on to do more than her share of housework. What the house always required, and had always got, was a devotion to its upkeep. I grudged every minute that took me away from reading, dreaming, writing poetry; I had no feeling for domesticity; no loyalty to the furniture or the rooms, particularly as they had been redone to my aunt's specifications. Would I have cared more lovingly for the house in its archaic state, with its improperly digested dreams of Europe, a Europe whose grandeur was unfashionable in the stripped-down, fast-moving, discarding temper of the times? Probably not, probably the horror would have been worse; dust, which became dirt and grime, settling into doilies and brocade rather than wall-to-wall carpeting and the fake fibers of the sectional. Probably it was better to destroy something charmless in its heart than something which, with care, might have maintained a tender innocence.

My mother and I destroyed the house. We didn't set fires or throw bottles at the mirrors or slit the surfaces of the furniture with furious knives. The house softened our limbs, congested our lungs so that we always felt we couldn't breathe or move enough to do what was required. We let things pile up. Every surface was covered with papers, some many years old, and we couldn't imagine how to begin to get rid of them. How could we contemplate repainting? Who would take the things off the walls, where would we put them while the painting was going on, how would we cover the furniture, and with what? Who would we hire? In my grandmother's time, she had only to lift a finger to get some man in the family to volunteer, but we no longer had those rights. In an odd burst of energetic employing, my mother hired the man who washed and waxed my glamorous aunt's linoleum to wash and wax our crumbling kitchen floor once every two weeks. We had to get ourselves out of bed by eleven on a Saturday morning to answer the door for him, to appear that we'd been up awhile, breakfasted, and were at work on our own tasks.

The living room became uninhabitable, so dusty that I was overcome with asthmatic attacks if I tried to sit there. So we didn't sit there. We stayed in the kitchen, where we would clear a little space on the table large enough for two plates. Not two together, one plate for my mother, then some papers, then an opening for a plate for me.

Upstairs in my pink room, the pink that age had darkened to the color of a particularly feminine bad luck, I allowed chaos to overcome me. I took my dirty sheets off the bed each week, but sometimes I didn't remake the bed for a day or two and slept on the bare mattress cover for a couple of nights, the sheets at the bottom of the bed in the brown paper from the Chinese laundry. When I was fifteen, a bird got into my closet from a hole in the wall near the chimney. I heard it struggling in there, and then I knew it had died. I waited a few weeks, then opened the door quickly, took out all my clothes, laid them on the chair, and never opened the closet again till it was time for college.

No change, even temporary, happened until I brought a man into the house. Or, of course, not a man, a boy, for I was still a girl.

My first boyfriend was an orphan. His parents had both died when he was in high school; he spent his last two years of high school in his sister's house. Did I choose him for myself or for my mother, or for both of us, to give to our diminished family unit a false sense of amplitude? Perhaps only an orphan could allow my mother's and my imagination the possibility of playing host, which we may have felt deprived of more than we knew.

Perhaps I chose him only because he chose me, a thing

that before this hadn't happened. He was older than I, a college man, hired by the nuns at my school (in a rare slippage of vigilance) to coach the debate club. Boys who'd gone to Jesuit high schools and colleges had got a training we, instructed by nuns to be quiet and deferential, simply had no access to. The Jesuit boys were trained to be killers, killers for Christ! They were encouraged to practice their arts on the Catholic Forensic League, where they regularly slashed their opponents to ribbons.

The one they hired as a coach, the one who later chose me, had no killer instinct. Rather he was orderly and formal. Formal without elegance, formal with the unlovable insecurity of someone who follows the rules without grasping the beauty of their original impulse, and cannot shape them to his nature or his taste, because he has no sense of either.

So in an age when boys were beginning to wear jeans and let their hair grow, he wore suits and visited the barber every week. His glasses were too heavy. His nose was too small, and his chin was weak. He was impatient without being quick, ingratiating with no natural sweetness. Still, he was male, and he wanted me. My mother took one look at him and thought her fears for me were over.

His college was in Jersey City, and he lived there in a fraternity house where he was tortured by the slovenliness of his housemates. Compared to them I guess, my mother's and my housekeeping failures must have seemed meliorable. He seemed glad to visit us, and we had so few visitors, none that seemed unwilling to leave. It was a long ride from Long Island to Jersey City. And so, my mother thought it sensible, natural, when he brought me home after our dates, to ask him to stay the night. Natural and proper, but it was neither natural nor proper for my mother to suggest that I give up my bedroom to him, and return once again to sleep beside her in my grandmother's old bed, the bed where I had slept before my father's death and then just afterward while our room was being fixed up. Not natural or proper for her to allow me to disappear with him upstairs for hours, under the feeble pretext that I was getting him towels from the linen closet. We lay down on my bed, across from the one that had been my mother's before my grandmother died and she took over that room, more convenient since she wouldn't have to climb the stairs. It was there that I was first touched by a man, there in my own girlhood bed, with my mother downstairs listening, if she chose, to the sounds we worked hard to muffle. And afterward I would lie down beside my mother, my body sweaty and lubricious from the upstairs activity that was extensive but stopped short of my virginity.

You see, I believe that house made people act strangely, made them come to decisions that could never be explained. My uncle on the porch, the family not telling my grandmother about the renovations, my mother allowing the house to decay, and now this, my partial violation on the premises that must have been protected and guarded by my grandmother's ghost. Was all this odd behavior an expression of a family taste for punishment, first of my uncle (punished for being male and good), then of me and my mother for intruding, then of my grandmother, in retaliation for her rigorous demands, and then her ghost? It was a house of punishment; it knew how to suggest punishment, and then to punish back.

My boyfriend was determined to try to bring the house back to order. He often stayed over on weekends, and, as we had when my grandmother and my aunt lived there, we spent all of Saturday cleaning. How my mother loved it: a man knocking himself out for her sake, and for mine. I didn't love it. He was my boyfriend. It was 1967. We should have been walking hand in hand singing Simon and Garfunkel, picnicking in Central Park, seeing Monet's *Water Lilies* in the Museum of Modern Art. Instead, the vacuum sounded its harsh, accusing roar and, like my aunt and grandmother, he found my housekeeping efforts inadequate and halfhearted. It was no wonder that, as soon as I got to college, I left him for a boy from southern Alabama I met at a be-in at the Sheep Meadow in Central Park.

The house demanded strength, but did not give it. It was not a loving house; it was a house that required service from a devoted lover, and perhaps, the limits of devotedness having been tested and reached, it would return regard. But we failed the house and it punished us and we, like whipped creatures, huddled against it, trying simply to survive. We needed a protector, and it had to be a mother or a man. After my grandmother's death, there were only two times when the ruin was staved off, and that was when I brought men in. What does that mean about my grandmother? That her implacability took the place of maleness? Did her qualities of unbending, perhaps merciless, rectitude give her the skeleton of a man, the shoulder span the house needed to keep itself alive, to breathe, and to be happy? My college years, the years between my first boyfriend and my first marriage, were the worst years for the house.

Before I left my poor first boyfriend, who was no match for everything that the be-in at the Sheep Meadow represented (the impromptu ease, the hopeful expansiveness), he'd painted my room yellow—buttercup yellow, cheerful as the rising sun—and helped me put up white curtains with yellow embroidery. I bought the curtains at JCPenney, already made up. They were too short for the windows of my bedroom, which had been there fifty years. He cleaned out the closet for me; I never mentioned the dead bird. It was bad enough to hear him complain about the dust-covered Halloween costumes, my eighth grade graduation or ninth grade dance dresses. If he saw a skeleton in the closet, tiny bird bones arranging themselves on the dust-covered floor, he didn't say anything. And he wasn't reticent in his complaints about the way he lived. What happened to the skeleton? Did it disappear, absorbed into less spectacular, less organic, more anonymous dust? Or was it never there? Was it simply the living metaphor of my terror and disgust, my inability to cope with something that anyone else would consider insignificant?

Ostensibly, I lived in my grandmother's house, now my mother's, for my first two years of college, but I was never there, or there with such reluctance, such rebellion, such unease that I never made a mark on the newly painted room. I slept on the floor of my friends' dorm rooms whenever I could; I slept in the beds of boys or men, calling my mother with false stories and false numbers. From my own newly yellow bedroom, next to the statue of my guardian angel and my father's picture of the Sacred Heart, I talked down friends on LSD trips and listened to my homosexual boyfriend's account of being taken to a party at Andy Warhol's Factory. By my junior year, I'd saved up enough money to pay for my own dorm room, and my mother reluctantly understood that as she had lost me anyway, she might as well give in. A week before I was to leave, she took a drunken fall and broke her leg in three places. With the heartlessness of desperation, I left the house anyway, left her in the care of the wife of one of her cousins. She was in a wheelchair for three months; I came home, furiously, resentfully, every Friday night, and spent the weekends that I thought would be my time for fun in the house that had become the house of a bedridden alcoholic. The dust piled high; the carpet shredded with age, the linoleum near the doorways disappeared, revealing a black underlayer, and I didn't lift a hand. I couldn't. In that house, I could do nothing but sleep.

Then I left the house; to go to graduate school in Syracuse. I came home, like other students, three or four times a year. Came home only to sleep and watch, helplessly, the house's degradation. My mother sealed off the top floor—she didn't want to pay to heat it—by taping plastic garment bags from the cleaners to each other to make a plastic curtain that hung from the ceiling to the floor of the stairway. It was hideous, but I didn't look at it, staying entirely out of the living room, sleeping in my mother's bed when I came home.

After graduate school I married a man who was a fanatical house cleaner. My mother's house, I'm sure, gave him pause about me. Like my first boyfriend, he spent all his visits cleaning the house. "It's hopeless," I said, "leave it alone." Let's not visit her, let's not come here, invite her to come to us, to our new house, the house you spend your spare time fixing, that you want me to decorate. I wanted to say to him: How can I decorate, I have no idea how to live, I have never bought a proper set of curtains, decisions of carpet and slipcover are as foreign, as terrifying, to me as space travel, and far, far more dangerous. Please, my love, my husband, my rescuer from the house that takes my breath, please understand. But he did not, and I left him. I left him for another man, but I couldn't tell my mother that. I told her, simply, my first husband and I were incompatible. She said, "I don't get it. All my life all I wanted was a man to clean up after me."

My second husband found the house a grief, but in the kindness of his nature, and his talent for avoiding the unpleasant, he pretended not to see what was unbearable to see. We went there rarely, and he, too, cleaned when we went, but without the furious, punitive vacuuming, the harsh application of fluids and polishes of my first boyfriend and my first husband. We brought a baby to the house, and I feared her contamination, but she was not contaminated, and my mother was happy, making a space on the table for the baby seat, letting the baby take her

naps beside her in the bed that had been my grandmother's, and hers, and shamefully, mine.

At seventy-five, my mother, whose drinking was beginning to interfere for the first time with her work, decided,
on my prodding, to retire. I bought her a house a block
away from me in the small town on the Hudson where I
lived. I was pregnant with my second child. We sold my
grandmother's house to people who lived two doors
away, a kind Italian family who had helped my mother
with shopping, who agreed to buy the house at a bargain
price in return for my not cleaning out the attic and the
cellar.

The mover was someone I'd gone to grammar school
with; he gave us a good price and sent his men to help us
pack. The week of the move, my mother-in-law became
fatally ill, and my husband had to be at her bedside in
Florida. I had to pack the house alone. I was constantly
nauseated with morning sickness that stretched into the
late afternoon, but I felt it was the right physical state to
go along with my feelings for the house.

As I was about to pack up a set of dishes that had been
bought by my aunt, I had a moment of inspiration. I'd
always hated those dishes; my grandmother's cheerful
blue-and-pink forget-me-not pattern had been put away
in favor of these, these horrible beige and white ones
with a gold rim, a pattern called Golden Wheat which my
aunt had got in box after box of Duz detergent. There was
a service for twelve. I took the set outside to the macadam

of the driveway and broke dish after dish. The sound was violent, and I was left with a small mountain of shards. Happily, I swept them into those black plastic garbage bags that always seem appropriate only for the bodies of the wartime dead. I left them on the sidewalk. I followed the moving van, driving with my mother and my baby, named for her, in my gray Honda Civic station wagon.

I went back to the house only once. The Italian family had completely transformed it. It was unrecognizable. They seemed happy. I was happy for them, and for myself, that the house had become something it was no longer possible for me to know.

GIRL CHILD
IN A
WOMEN'S WORLD

THERE WERE FOUR daughters and a son. The girls were called Constance, Monica, Sabena, Brenda: not an unexceptional name among them. The brother was called J.V., as if his abashment over the distinction of his sisters' names made him feel he had no right to anything but initials. To him, in his army uniform, I took my first steps. He was home from Korea and rarely after that.

My mother knew Mrs. Kirk from church. She agreed to look after me for modest payments. At first my mother thought that her own mother would look after me. But my grandmother didn't look after any of the other grandchildren and was afraid to cause a family rift. Perhaps, too, my grandmother refused to look after me as a way of highlighting and punishing my father's failure to hold a job.

Why did my mother hire Mrs. Kirk? She was a slattern, with missing front teeth and witch hair. Her housedresses were ripped and loose. I am forgetting though that on those rare occasions when she appeared in public—and this, of course, is how my mother would have known her—she put in her bridge and pinned up her hair. She put on a corset and wool dress with a belt. She appeared presentable: she changed, but nothing ever changed about the house. The darkness of her house was in itself a kind of architecture. What could have made a house so dark? Perhaps it was the bushes that grew up, dense, shaped, around the windows. And it was the blackout shades, pulled down in early afternoon. Still, there must have been some place, some part of a room, a corner of a hall-way, where light struck, where a yellowish patch, tran-sected by striped shadows, came to rest on a wooden floor. Some moment of a day when the windows were let open that the house must have been not dark. But I do not remember such a place or time.

I remember heavy furniture. I remember a picture above a chair: fat Romantic girl children with long, black wavy hair, improperly mature, drapery fallen away to show voluptuous pectoral flesh. I remember a long table in the dining room that reached from one end of the room to the other, and the word *mahogany*, which Mrs. Kirk wanted me to know indicated seriousness and expense. I thought from listening to her that there were only two kinds of wood: maple and mahogany. Maple was for the girls' room. It was the wood of youth.

The house faced on to Scranton Avenue, a busy street. On its right side was a Howard Johnson's, on its left a harsh, disturbing vacant lot. So they bounded their prop-erty by hedges. A slice in one of the hedges became a path made up of large, uneven stones ending at a grape-colored shingled porch. The flowers in the garden were night flowers. I remember nothing springlike, nothing vibrant. Daffodils and tulips cannot have been planted there. I think of tiger lilies, threatening with open mouths. And most of all chrysanthemums, which I would pick too short and ruin, and be scolded for. I wasn't told not to pick the flowers, but I was never given scissors. There was general disappointment when I produced my stunted handful, graceless as damaged children, all distressing heads. The response suggested that they believed I ought to have done better. With a sigh, Mrs. Kirk would indicate the trash can and sweep out, banging the wooden screen door like a diva. She would return with a bouquet, ascetic yet luxuriant. She would lay it down on the chipped yellow counter. She would reach below into a cabinet and bring out a roll of waxed paper. The sound of the tearing waxed paper thrilled me in my shame. She would twist the paper into a crescent or funnel shape and slip the flowers in. "Now that's nice for your mother," she would say.

Sometimes my mother would come to get me; sometimes it would be my father. My mother would be driving; my father would arrive on foot. My mother would drive up the driveway, a pebbled strip on the side of the property that bordered the vacant lot. There was no way I could tell that she was coming until the second that I heard her car whirling up pebbles as she drove in.

She didn't like to get out of the car. She honked her horn. Mrs. Kirk felt the honor of my mother's professional life had rubbed off on her—my mother was a secretary—and so she was glad to bring me to the car. Leaving me, she left each day a report on my behavior. She and my mother were at war against my secret vice, the private experience of sexual pleasure, which I probably discovered out of the drowning boredom of my days with Mrs. Kirk. "She's been very bad at it," Mrs. Kirk would say, or "She's done quite a number of it today." I never remember her saying that I had been good. A sense of badness like a rinse of dirty water covered me on the ride home. My mother was tight-jawed and angry. Only after dinner, when she listened to the radio, when she ironed and drank coffee or iced drinks, did she flower again to the mother I had yearned for all day: fragrant, contained, light, compact. The opposite of life at Mrs. Kirk's, the mother in her crisp delicious clothes who adored me.

My father would arrive on foot. With him, there was a signal I could hope for. I could sit on the front porch and hear, as he walked on the sidewalk in front of the house, still hidden by the hedges, the sound of the coins that clinked together in his pocket. Before I would see him, I would hear the sound of change. *Change.* And things would change. I would run down the path to meet him. He would lift me in one arm and carry me, tipped against his body. He carried a briefcase in his other hand: he had to hold that as well as me.

In the time I sat waiting for my father, I was a sponge

saturated by longing. I was only one quality, one faculty: I yearned. The clinking sound of his arrival was deliverance. Had I been older, or a visionary child like the Fatima children I later prayed to, I could have prostrated myself on the ground, not before my father, but before the universe for containing within itself the possibility of such complete deliverance, such perfect relief. Mrs. Kirk never reported my badness to my father, partly, I think, because she guessed that he wouldn't believe her, partly because he was male, and partly because she couldn't place him in the world. Who was this man who didn't earn the family money, whose work life she had no proof of (there was none) except his carrying a briefcase, who took days off simply to have his daughter near him, simply to be at home with a child?

I'd guessed that Mrs. Kirk didn't respect my father, but one day she made it clear. I said, "My father is very intelligent." She looked surprised. "Your father?" she said. "It's your mother with the brains. Your mother's as smart as a whip."

I knew then that Mrs. Kirk stood for complete misunderstanding of the world. She didn't understand even that my family was built on a fervid schizophrenic dualism in regard to money. My father's job was to be an intellectual. He wrote unpublishable articles full of references to Charles Péguy and the Desert Fathers. But he didn't earn a cent. His role in our financial life was to create debt; it spread around him like a pool of ink. His plans for magazines, for lecture series, required always an initial small outlay of capital. His only resource was my mother. He would lose the fifty, the one hundred dollars she had for-warded and she would swear never again to trust him with a penny. During these periods, he would have to beg her each morning for the money that he needed to get through the day. "I only want my carfare," I would hear him saying and she would shout, "For what? Where are you going that's worth it? If you spent the carfare looking for a job I wouldn't mind. But I won't give you money for another thing that doesn't get you a good job."

I had a surprisingly firm idea of what a good job would entail. It would be in an office, a room so thor-oughly well lighted that there no failure would lodge, a place where there would be cigarette smoke, cigar smoke, the sound of voices and of doors opening and shutting. A place that began activity at a certain hour and ceased it at a time equally well determined. My father would put on his hat and leave that dry, visibly lovable world. And take the train. To us. To me. To get me at the Kirks'. It never occurred to me that if he got a "good job," my mother would stay home. Her life was in the world, as mine would be. As his was. As the Kirks', father and mother, was not. And so the notion of "a good job," that desirable entity my father couldn't seem to grasp, didn't have to do in my mind with a change in our manner of living. It was more a visual idea: an area for my father to inhabit, a new way of moving. His inability to take his place in the world of work, so glamorous for my mother and her boss, a lawyer whom she worshiped, didn't cause either my mother or me to suspect my father's superior-ity. He failed, but he was not inferior: neither of us had trouble holding, simultaneously, these two thoughts in our mind.

I knew that even though it brought him money, Basil Kirk's job did not take up desirable space. He worked at night in the post office. When I saw him, it was only to observe him sluggishly proceeding through the late afternoon that was morning to him, his jaw, underslung like a bulldog's, covered with a stubble that represented to me all that I must keep away from in the world of men. He moved in the kitchen in the same way that the wet wash arrived, a part of domestic life, but unformed and unrecognizable in its historic function. The shirts would eventually be dried, pressed, and hung on hangers; Basil would eventually shave, dress, and go out to his job, but I would never witness either transformation and my disbelief that either would happen made me recoil from the steaming laundry and from the man who had the name of husband, father, but who slept all day.

Basil's diurnal imbalance was only one more proof to me of the wrongness of the Kirks' life. I put some of this wrongness down to the fact that they were German. Basil wasn't even Catholic, he was Presbyterian, and although Mrs. Kirk's family traced their allegiance to the Church back for centuries, I found it unconvincing. They were neither Irish nor Italian, like the other people in the parish. I had some notion of Germany's *northernness,* and I had heard contemptuously spoken the name Martin Luther. Martin Luther, who had ruined everything for everyone through pride, through his refusal to have bent the knee. From the pulpit, triumphantly, priests would tell the story of Martin Luther's last words: "It is so difficult to live a Catholic life but so beautiful to die a Catholic death." It didn't occur to me then to doubt the truth of the story: I couldn't have imagined, then, that lies came from the altar, but how can that story have been true? Luther wouldn't have had Catholic sympathizers with him at his deathbed, and the Protestants, knowing he had already turned into an icon, the very people who'd arranged that there should be a death mask, would have kept the story quiet, even if it had occurred.

The time that Mrs. Kirk took care of me began less than five years after the end of the war, yet for me Germany was Luther and not Hitler. In my dreams, men in brown uniforms shaved the heads of naked women who stood only in their high heels in the center of the town to be punished for a crime I had no way of naming. I treasured a story of French war children hoarding, for months, a stick of chewing gum, a single chocolate coin which the oldest would keep in her pocket and allow the younger to touch, with a moistened index finger which they could lick one time each day. But I didn't connect them with Luther. For Mrs. Kirk's ancient father, whom I was instructed to call Grandpa Haubrecht, sat all day in the dark house, himself like a dark stone figure, silent until he broke into a German tirade which was explained to me to be about his hatred of Martin Luther.

All day he sat like stone. Except to light his pipe, he was immobile. He wore a brown suit, peppered with little holes like grapeshot made from the sparks that fell out of his pipe. His teeth were broken down like rocks and brownish yellow. He wore brown bootlike shoes, clean but dull, unlike the hard shoes I had seen on men, hard shoes that took a shine. Mrs. Kirk told my mother about his night crimes. My mother was her confidante. He would escape the house at midnight, Mrs. Kirk would tell my mother, wearing only his underwear, which he slept in. (This, to me, was the most shocking detail: what kind of person wouldn't own pajamas?) He would find his way to the Lutheran church where he would shout, in German, speeches about Luther of the purest filth. Luckily, Mrs. Kirk told my mother, the police who came to get him didn't understand German.

It was with Grandpa Haubrecht that I had my first false human relations. Much of my life was made up of false seeming, but the falsity was unconnected to a specific human being. It consisted of my having to pretend I was a child. I knew my family was odd, but I was sure of our distinction as a unit; my parents' superiority to other, ordinary parents was clear to me. And in my connection to them, my differentness could be distinction: at least the possibility was there. But on my own in the world, I knew my differentness only as a hindrance. My interests were not appropriate to my state in life. I hated coloring books, sandboxes, games that involved running, chasing, hiding, being safe on base. I thought comic books were ridiculous, except for one, about a buxom model called Katy Keene. And I liked *Nancy* because I was interested in her aunt. I enjoyed watching movies with my parents, the movies they liked, with real, grown-up, and beautifully dressed people, not mice and ducks and pigs and farmers chasing each other to no end. I liked lives of the saints and fairy tales with European illustrations. At four, I liked carrying one of my mother's used black leather pocketbooks: the smell of her powder lingered in the inside compartments; she gave me a lace-edged handkerchief and a nearly used-up lipstick to keep inside the bag. Mrs. Kirk hated to see me with it. One day she presented me with a small red plastic child's pocketbook with a hard plastic snowman glued to the front. "I thought it was time you got rid of that black monstrosity," she said. Monstrosity. The word made me unable to love the object for another second. I saw the virtues of the new pocketbook: it was easier to carry and more colorful. The smiling snowman wished me well. I understood that if I carried that child's pocketbook, I could be perceived as an ordinary child. If I could have about me one of the objects that was a sign of ordinary childhood, I could appear to be the thing I had no interest in actually becoming and yet yearned to *seem* to be.

The only kind of child I was interested in being was the child princess of fairy tale. I liked the clothes; my dream was always to be dressed in full, long skirts. The overalls, the limp, thin dresses and dark wool socks I was condemned to wear were a torment. More: they concealed my real nature. I knew who I was. But it appeared to be impossible that I should move in the world in a way that reflected my true (royal) identity. My second choice, therefore, was to appear to be generous, self-sacrificing, kind. In the saints' lives I adored and in the brief, unsatisfactory glimpses I had of childhood moral heroism in movies, a common theme seemed to be struck: the union of the very young and the very old. This seemed to work well for everyone. I was particularly impressed by the misty gaze of observing adults in movies as they stood watching, touched and grateful for the sight. I decided I would cultivate Grandpa Haubrecht. I didn't like him, I was frightened of him, but that was all the better: the conversion for the both of us would be satisfying. Real.

He sat smoking in his hard chair. His eyes were dead; they looked ahead of him at nothing. They were the stone eyes of statues I had seen and feared. I sat down at his feet. He didn't look at me. I kissed his knee. The material of his pants was stiff; the bone beneath it gave no sign of liveliness. He didn't move or respond. I kissed the knee again. Nothing. Silence. Smoking. The gaze into dead air. I was beginning to feel desperate. I was a child; he was an old man: something was supposed to be felt. I learned the bully's desperate timing. I knocked on his knee ten, twelve, fifteen times and kissed again. Nothing. He smoked his pipe. He never looked at me.

I understood that I was not a child.

The Kirk girls weren't girls at all. Their youth was something I had missed, so I could not believe in it. They locked themselves into my vision fully formed, voluptuous, adult as movie stars, American. They had been cleansed of all their parents' mistakes about the world. None of the errors of the house were theirs.

How old were they? I now have no way of knowing. I

can place the older two, Constance and Monica, by their public lives. And by their photographs, Constance in her WAVE uniform, Monica in her cap and gown. Mrs. Kirk took care of me for five years; over that time there must have been, for the girls, some process of maturing, of aging, which I could have witnessed. But of course I did not. No child records gradual, incremental change; the Kirk girls were set for me in varying stages of nonchildhood, although for most of the time I spent in her house, Sabena must have been a child. Like me. Or like me, pretending.

I knew Constance only in uniform. She was away in Washington. In the WAVEs. The WAVEs, a name combining natural and military romance. And then one time, she arrived home a fiancée. Her mother and sisters came together in a spasm of unified action. They carried the dining room table out to the garage. They painted trim and vacuumed the upholstery. They made dishes out of foods that before this never had occurred to them: crabmeat, pecans. I was under their feet and I knew well enough to keep out of the way. I was happy to sit on the couch and stare up at the crepe paper bell suspended from the ceiling. Miraculous. I had seen it on the dining room table before the table had been taken out to the garage. It had lain inert, in the shape of a boot like Italy, flat, the color of gray cardboard. Then Brenda had shown me how it worked. She moved it on its hinge: it opened and became white; fragile, full, like spring snow on a branch of apple blossom, like the dresses of the princesses of whose company I knew myself to be. Brenda promised me that she would ask her mother to give me the bell to take home when the party was over. So I was content to sit in the dark living room and worship the crepe paper bell, a sacred object like the rotting hats of the dead cardinals that hung suspended from the ceiling of Saint Patrick's. Only better. I would one day own the object of my veneration. One day I would touch it. One day I would cause it to fold on itself and disappear, or to appear from nothing at my bidding. At my will and at my touch.

Or was this bell, and this activity, not for Constance's engagement party, but for Monica's? It is possible that Constance married apart from the family, quietly and militarily, and came home uniformed with her uniformed fiancé (now husband) only to tell the news. I know that at some point she came home with a baby, and I hated that. I understood that the Kirks saw me as inhabiting the same estate as their nephew, an estate apart from them. I wanted, above all, for them to see that I was linked to them in the exacting enterprise of femaleness that took up and exhausted them. I wanted to be one of them. I wanted to be of the party that dressed and undressed not merely for comfort, the party of perfume that smelled not quite fresh, of the butt ends of cosmetics collected in a glass dish on a bureau, of hair taken from hairbrushes and dropped into the toilet, left unflushed along with the extravagantly half-smoked cigarette with lipstick around its tip. The dark party of the female sex.

But now I am only talking about Monica. It was

Monica's physical life that drove the family. Not her beauty, it was not that that drove them, and not force, but her appeal. They were devoted to the response she could evoke in men. They served it; they were happy to.

I saw what Monica could do at firsthand once. Two young men came to the door selling subscriptions to magazines. Mrs. Kirk wasn't home; it was Sabena, Brenda, Monica, and me. Monica was in charge. She invited the young men in. They sat down in the living room. She brought them iced tea, made with mint that grew by the side of the house, beneath the dripping hose connection. The young men spoke about their magazines. *Reader's Digest,* they said. *Cue. Look. Life.* Monica listened as if she were from a backward country that had never known such things as magazines. She stared absently. She gave nothing out. She was a kind of receptor: she took in their desire. All three of them seemed stupefied. After a while, both the young men asked her to dinner. The smaller one, who had broken out in a sweat (his hair was already thinning), said: "I'll spend all the money I earned today and take you for a steak dinner." The taller, thinner, shier one said, "It'll only be beans from me, but it'll be from the heart." I didn't know whether he was poorer than the other one, or simply convinced that no amount of effort on his part would make a difference. He was clearly overmastered by his colleague; he carried the sample case and entered the door behind him. I knew I wanted the tall, thin, defeated one to win Monica, but I knew he wouldn't. In the end, it never came to anything, because my father arrived, and in an uncharacteristic assertion of traditional male authority, he drove the two young men from the house. They got up, ashamed as if they had been interrupted in the transgression they had only dreamed of. Monica seemed grateful to my father, and relieved. I didn't know why; I knew that she had made what happened happen.

She was languid, she was indolent, yet she caused things to occur around her. At her suggestion, her mother and sisters began making bandages for the Cancer Guild, then horses out of braided rags for crippled children. When her interest lagged, the activity would stop: the work would be left out for a while; cloth, pins, and scissors would be kept ready on the sideboard, then they would one day not be there.

She had dull, grayish, carnal eyes and full lips that didn't smile or laugh readily. To the right of her lower lip there was a perfect mole. She wore sweaters and skirts; no clothing she put on her body ever stood out from it: even her garments could not resist her. When I first knew her, she was still wearing a Catholic school uniform. How frustrating it must have been for the nuns, who had invented such outfits to make a young girl's sexual allure seem to be beside the point, that on Monica the harsh pleats melted into one another and the stiff bodice over the stiffened blouse lay down, softened themselves, made themselves passive victims on Monica's wonderful breasts.

I didn't think that she was beautiful. There was something fetid about her slow-movingness; even as I was drawn to it, I didn't want to be. I preferred Brenda, who was blond, quick, edgy, tomboyish. She liked to wear what we then called dungarees, and plaid shirts, and she was generally in a position of service to her mother, her sisters, to my mother, who paid her to clean our house on Saturdays. She even served me: she would carry me piggyback down the stairs; she was the only one in the family who ever stirred herself to find anything that might interest me to do. When she carried me, I noticed that her sweat smelled like chicken noodle soup. I admired my own power of association. I thought that she would make the perfect cowgirl; I cast her in the part of Annie Oakley, one of my heroes at the time. I feared that she would never marry. Perhaps I hoped that she would not.

I would be glad to see Brenda today, but I would run from Sabena. She excelled in finding me in my avid sinning. She would discover me; she would watch me for a few seconds before letting me know that she was there. She would smile horribly. "I'm going to tell my mother. I have no choice," she would say. I would nod miserably, knowing no act of mine could be effectual. It now occurs to me that probably I could have bribed her. She had the perfect nature for a blackmailer. Interested in the crime herself, accurate in her timing, she would never have stopped watching me. But she liked luxuries—Dutch coffee candies, Tangee lipstick she was not allowed, Evening in Paris perfume in small dark blue bottles. I could have turned thief for her, if I'd thought of it. I could have stolen from my father to keep her mouth shut.

Monica became engaged to George who was a Greek, a banker. He was shorter than her by inches; his hair was

stuck to his head with horrifying grease. I didn't understand how he had won her; but I knew he did. I had my
evidence. I found, stuck behind one of the pillows of the
couch, a letter she had written to him. "Dear Darling," it
began.

I don't remember what it said after that; those two
words told me everything that I needed to know. It was
the final proof I needed that I was a creature so different
from Monica that I would never have a chance at an
experience resembling hers. I knew that you said "dear,"
or you said "darling." I knew that you did not say both.
No feeling I would ever have for any man would cause
me to make that error. And I felt that, knowing that, I
would not be chosen, for something of what men chose
in Monica was that indolence, that failure of alertness that
would cause her to yoke two such improper words.

At Monica's wedding, I left early with my father. We
left before the cake. That was my favorite part of the wedding: getting my father to leave. No one noticed us, or
almost no one: Mrs. Kirk saw, but she didn't care enough
about either of our presences to mind. I have no memory
of Monica the bride or her sisters, the flowerlike atten-
dants. I don't remember food or music. I remember leaving with my father. Down the path through the split in
the hedge.

My mother stayed till the end. She brought me home
a piece of cake. She told me to put it under my pillow.
That way, she said, I'd see in my dreams the face of the
man I was meant to marry.

PLACES TO PLAY

As a child, I was not good at playing, which means I was a failure at the duties of my state in life. The phrase "Go and play" had for me the ring of a sentence handed down by a mercilessly careless magistrate. The phrase which marked my deliverance was this: "All right, I guess you might as well go read that book."

The sentence of doom, "Go and play," was not spoken in my parents' voice. My parents (whose child I, after all, was, the only kind of child they had the strength for) never suggested alternatives to reading. And because I was almost always reading, there was nothing for them to suggest.

When I read, it didn't matter that I was only masquerading as a child. There was no falseness in my position as a reader. If I lost myself in the fates of virgin martyrs or fairy princesses, if I was Napoleon or one of the Salem witches, there was nothing shameful in the shiftiness of my identity. It was expected that ordinary human beings lost themselves in that way, it was only the proof of a serious or ardent nature, not the evidence of a crook's sleight of hand.

It must be because they felt cheated, or stolen from, that a certain kind of adult so disliked me. These non-readers were practical people, whose attention was on the visible, what could be fixed and made to run. What did they feel I was stealing, or making a false claim to? Like one of the false Anastasias. To them, I was stealing the royal identity of the child. Or was it the opposite: that, appearing to be a child, I thought the kingdom of adult-hood my birthright and didn't want to earn my place in its municipality?

Or perhaps they merely hated me because when they laid eyes on me I was so often so obviously bored. And what is less endurable than the countenance of a bored child? To both adults and to other children. Because children didn't like me either. Children don't understand boredom; it's not really an emotion, like rage or joy. It's a state whose very evenness is a torment; it's not a response to a stimulus, it's the emptiness taking up the space where stimulus should be, a stagnant pool where what is longed for is the crash and roar of breakers.

But I was regularly bored, because I thought that what other children considered worthwhile pastimes were completely ridiculous. I hated the idea of games. Hide-and-seek made me feel both hopeless and entrapped. Why would I position myself in one or another dark place, crouched and blinded, waiting to pounce or to be pounced upon. And for what? For what? That was, always to me, the question in games other children seemed to enjoy playing. I couldn't countenance such an expendi-ture of energy for such a paltry result. Running tired me,

I was afraid to climb, I couldn't catch a ball because I feared being hit by it in the face or stomach.

Nothing I liked to read about, even, had to do with rapid movement, action, or adventure. I liked fairly tales and saints' lives. Best were stories of women of virtue, whose virtue made them more desirable to a man who perhaps began his connection with them reluctantly. My two favorites were *The Swan Prince* and the life of Saint Elizabeth of Hungary. *The Swan Prince* was about a princess whose three prince brothers were turned into swans by a jealous witch. In order to free her brothers, she had to knit them shirts made of nettles, and then throw the shirts onto the bodies of her flying bird brothers. At the appointed time, she had still not finished the last sleeve of the last shirt for the youngest, and he was restored to humanity with one arm and one wing. But she, for her heroism, was chosen by the king's son for his own.

St. Elizabeth of Hungary was a queen who defied her tyrant husband by hiding bread in her skirts for starving peasants. Her husband caught her at the door and threatened her with death if he found her carrying bread against his orders. She loosened her skirt, and behold, there was not bread, but roses! Her husband, seeing the transformation, fell to his knees before his wife.

My play didn't involve reenacting the narratives of these stories. What I liked to do in the realm, the area, of what could even generously be thought of or called play, had its source in what I read. But it was an aura, a tonality rather than a road map that I was after. It was as if I were trying to surround myself with fabric that could dress my dreams. I wanted an atmosphere that I could enter—and do what? I would have said, at the time, *pretend,* a word that sounded better, more descriptive to me, than the overloose word *play.*

My props in these dramas—or operettas, really—of pretending began with a collection of old birthday cards that had been sent to me or to my mother. I stored them in a cardboard box with a pattern of ribbons and roses embossed into its surface. I sat in my play corner, took the cards out of the box, and looked at them. That was what I did: I looked.

My play corner was the corner of my father's study, in a part of the room otherwise unusable because it was only an expanse of floor that stretched out, like an isthmus, from a wide closet door. In the closet were my father's clothes, fragrant with his outside life, the life he lived apart from me and from my mother. Gabardine and cigars, a mix that was the sign of a bracing, foreign, and necessary maleness. On the floor of the closet, alongside my father's shoes, was my toy box: a tin rectangle, two feet by four, painted in a circus design in circus colors.

That I was given only this inadequate space for play explains, perhaps, or at least provides a lively metaphor for, why I didn't have more appetite for play, why I didn't think it was important. It was because my parents didn't think it was important. But how could they, given who they were, at the point of their lives when I entered?

I was the child of parents old enough to be my grand-parents. My mother was forty-one when I was born; my father was fifty-seven. My mother was a cripple, a victim of polio. My father, although we didn't take it into account (I couldn't, for I didn't know it), was suffering from heart disease. He'd had heart attacks in his forties. They were serious people, my parents. Not, in some Protestant way, having to do with either respectability or ambition. In my mother's case, seriousness sprang from the necessity that money be earned, and an appetite for and pleasure in her work. My mother was a secretary, and I think she loved herself most, and maybe most purely, for being good at what she could earn money at.

And my father; my father was a writer, trying to write the truth for a world in danger of perishing. Trying, also, to get published, a task nearly as impossible as purifying the corrupt world.

So because of who they were, because of age and physical condition, they didn't think of making it a part of their day to take me outside (they were too tired, or their limbs too weak), they couldn't throw a ball for me, or give me a boost so I could climb a tree, or run behind me so I could learn to ride a bicycle, or defend me from a bully, or at least teach me to defend myself. That was part of it, certainly, but at the time when I was at the center of their lives they were simply people who believed that what was important in life happened indoors and had to do with words.

Whatever the reasons, the fact was that the places I was happiest playing were spaces carved out of the rooms where my parents worked.

My father's work produced no product. I observed it in or through a darkness as I watched him sitting at his desk, in the room which had two windows but which never seemed to get the benefits of light.

To describe my father's office properly, I must tell the truth about our family life. We called the room his office but really it was his bedroom. It should have been mine. I can imagine how things developed; they probably evolved, as strange things often do in families, from quite a normal beginning, a domestic accommodation to an event whose sources are practical. I can understand that when I was brought home from the hospital, my parents put my bassinet in the room with them, so they could be available to respond to my nighttime cries. The bassinet would have been replaced by a crib. This might have been the time to move my father's desk and typewriter out of what had been his office before my birth, to find another place for the phone. To make his room my room. But where would we have put my father's desk and typewriter? There was no other room, and he had to have a place in which to do his work.

What I don't know is when the single bed was moved into that office. Was it there before I was born? Was it the place guests slept? Why wasn't I put in the single bed, leaving a corner of the room as my father's study? Why, instead, when it was time for me to move from the crib to a bed was a cot moved into the master bedroom? And why was I put to bed, not in my own cot, but in the marriage bed? I know that I was hard to get to sleep, that I was famous for being "a bad sleeper." Was that the reason that I took my father's place beside my mother? Or was it a good arrangement for everyone? Was my father happier beside his desk and typewriter than beside my mother's body? Certainly, I was happier beside her than in the hard army cot with the mattress made (frighteningly, for my too active imagination) of horsehair. Every time I lay on it, I had to think of a scalped horse, all skin, having given up its liveliness, its luster, for my sake.

From the dark corner in front of the closet door, I watched my father's back. I heard him type and shuffle papers. On the wall above his desk was a print of Holbein's Thomas More. A dark man, with dark hair and brooding eyes, penetrating and accusing, wearing a red cloak and a gold chain. In the oak of my father's desk were dark whorls, lines which, when no one was around, I traced with the point of my pencil, following them somewhere, nowhere, until I gave up with my fruitless journey, circular and without end.

In my corner, I surrounded myself with objects that involved lightness because I was trying to construct a world of lightness. A world which would appeal to nobody I knew well, a world I understood to be inferior in its overly accessible desirability, to the world I believed was important. The world of grave-eyed Thomas More. I wanted a world I could sense would be unpalatable to a maturely developed taste. But I didn't need to have that kind of taste yet; I could stay in the world of pastels, ringlets, hoop skirts, pansies, daisies, rosebuds, not the full-throated, full-bloomed, deep-colored mature flower, but pinkish baby-faced blossoms, fragile except that my universe didn't admit to any element forceful enough to cause damage.

To create this world, whose cardinal virtue was prettiness, I began by spreading the birthday cards on the part of the floor covered by a strip of charcoal-colored carpet. Once that was done I could disappear and become— what exactly was it that I hoped I could become? One of the girls in crinolines and ruffled pantaloons and lace-up slippers? One of the girls in yellow bonnets on the birthday card that said "To a Special Girl"?

Still keeping the cards on the floor, I would take my toys out of the circus-colored box. Cinderella dancing in her pink dress with the prince, a toy I could wind up and watch spin. Alice with the Mad Hatter in the center of a dolls' tablecloth. A wooden box of yellow, violet, periwinkle-colored chalks, and an accompanying square of glass on which I made a colored surface that would turn whatever it was placed over just that magic color, but which still could be seen through. Slippers, only for play, impossible to walk in, made of knotted gold yarn with satin soles. Squares of silk—rejected from the linings of the coats my grandmother made—that could be transformed into a veil or gown. A china tea set, miniature, white with pale forget-me-nots.

I became not a figure or a character, but a color and a texture, soft, edgeless, inviting. I became an atmosphere. I lost my history, my face.

Happily faceless in a world that was made up of tones, or one tone only (the sweetest, the simplest), I sat silent, feeling the need to express nothing while at his desk my father pounded out words for which, like Thomas More, I knew he might be martyred.

On the floor, a faceless girl, a girl involved in prettiness, I created a world impossible to my family's imagination: A world without martyrdom. A world without heroics. A world where nothing was at stake.

In my father's office, I could always lift my eyes and see him, sitting in the light of his green-shaded lamp, his fingers on the typewriter keys, his pictures on the walls, his cigars, his books, his clothing. Playing beside my working mother, I inhabited a radically different atmosphere.

My mother's office was outside the house, and not really her office, but her boss's. She had made what were, for the time, unusual working arrangements so that she could keep her job and still have time with me. She worked every day from twelve to six. My admirable mother, never more desirable than when her maternity was attached to her work life, never more mine than when she was leaving for the office.

Her relationship with her boss was, I believe, the most wholly satisfying of her life. Must I reduce this beauty to a type, to an identifiable phenomenon in the history of workers and of class? Because, certainly, I suppose it is possible to say my mother was oppressed. She should have been encouraged to go to law school; she was one of those secretaries of whom it was rightly said she knew more than most lawyers. She, of course, did not believe she knew more than her boss, and she may not have. I have no reason to think that he was anything but superb in his work; certainly, he prospered, financially and politically. He was a German farmboy and worked the land when Long Island was potato farms. Exhausted, and with dirt under his nails, he took the trolley into Brooklyn Law School. He married a pretty, genuinely sweet blond woman and had two blond children. He entered politics as a Republican, and was twice elected town supervisor. He was connected with the building of Jones Beach; in his office, there was a picture of himself and Robert Moses, and underneath them, in white architects' printing, the words *The Jones Beach Jetty*.

In all the years that I looked at that photograph, of the two bald, serious-faced men, I had no idea what a jetty was, or why it might be important. It seemed a male word, a word I would have no possible access to. But I knew that photograph was the emblem of importance. In a way that frightened and excited me, it gave a glimpse into what power in the world might be.

My mother and her boss had a perfect working partnership. He called her "Miss Anne," as did his wife and children. Does that imply condescension, even a hint of the plantation? Does it matter? They were happy. They worked well. They were famous, in a limited circle, to be sure, but nevertheless the fame was real, for the excellence of their joint work.

The office was on the second floor of a brick building whose history I knew. It had belonged to another old German farmer, who had made a fortune selling his land. This man was dead before I was born, but I saw him clearly, because of the stories I had heard. He was fat and bald, and he wore red suspenders. His wife had died; he had an only daughter who was, according to my mother, "unfortunate looking." He consorted with prostitutes; he may have brought prostitutes into the house, before his daughter's eyes. The daughter went mad, "sex mad," my mother said; when a man came near her, she jumped on him.

The building, once owned by the late father, now owned in trust for the daughter (my mother's boss was her guardian), was made of brick. On the ground floor was a drugstore. Its name was written in the florid script of the Whelan's chain, a *W* like a wave, an *S* like the trailing of a peignoir in a thirties screwball comedy.

My mother was beloved in that drugstore; her presence was always treasured by shopkeepers; she was the master of the casual encounter, she imparted a crispness, a respectability, a sense at once of purpose and of play to her transactions. Storekeepers could feel only blessed and enlarged by this. We called the pharmacist "Doc." Doc was a large, dark, thickly moustached Jew. He and his small birdlike wife wore white jackets and labored behind a high counter that was flanked by two glass vats filled with liquids, one red, one blue, which seemed to me to have arrived on that counter straight from the Arabian Nights. I couldn't imagine what those colored liquids could have been, but I had infinite respect for them, awe even, and I loved staring at them for their dosage of pure color.

And I loved it when my mother would make a purchase at the drugstore, a purchase of cosmetics, or shampoo, or most importantly talcum powder. My parents had no financial margin, so these purchases could not be casual. My mother would consult me: would we buy April Showers powder or Cashmere Bouquet? Now I understand that both were inexpensive, and probably undistinguished. But to me, then, the difference between them was monumental, and was suggested by the difference of the color of their tin containers. April Showers was a light turquoise with a shadow of raspberry-colored leaves and blossoms; Cashmere Bouquet was powder pink (I try to think what was meant to be suggested by a bouquet of cashmere: wool flowers? What was desirable about that? Only, perhaps, the juxtaposition of two valuables—cashmere, standing for luxury, bouquet, hinting of opulence). I would struggle over this decision: April Showers was nature, Cashmere Bouquet the glamours of civilization. I was never sure, when I had chosen, that I had chosen right.

One year, there was a scandal at the drugstore. Doc left his little sparrow of a wife and took up with the voluptuous Ruth: an Anita Ekberg type who wore backless leopard-print high heels, hoop earrings the size of doughnuts, and orange lipstick that went over the natural line of her lips. My mother was in conflict: should she refuse to patronize Doc, on the grounds of his misbehavior, his betrayal of his lawful wife, or should she take the line that it wasn't her business and since they weren't Catholic, the question of marriage wasn't the same for them. She took the latter position, although she never failed to criticize Ruth after we left. "That is a very vulgar woman," she said to me, on her way upstairs to her chaste office. When she said that, I imagined that what she meant was that Ruth did not bathe.

While my mother talked to Doc, or Ruth, or Mac, the assistant, I wandered around the store. Here, too, I was looking for clues about what being a real, a desirable woman might entail, although it wouldn't have occurred to me to connect what I was after with men and desire, only their admiration and an impulse to protect. I looked at the one shelf of costume jewelry: there was a pair of blue crystal beads I must have examined for five years. I looked at the shades of nail polish and lipstick: Windsor Rose, Real Red, Cherries in the Snow. I looked at the names of perfumes: Command Performance, My Sin. Then I looked at my mother and at Ruth and I knew that nothing that I wanted for myself had anything to do with them. I spent a long time in front of an ad for hairspray that had pictures of two women, a blond with long, wind-blown hair, and a brunet in a chignon. I was anguished by not being blond, and always looking for dark models who might give me hope. The brunet in the chignon looked soulful, European; she had suffered, she had understood a great deal, but she had not been marred or rendered less valuable by the experience. Under the blond were the words *the natural look,* and under the brunet, *the sophisticated look.* I told my father I wanted the sophisticated look. He glared at me: "Don't ever let me hear anybody call you sophisticated," he said. I felt hopeless again, and crushed.

Every day, my mother, despite her crippling polio, had to walk up the wide wooden stairs—there must have been twenty of them—to get to the office where she worked. She dreaded it; she talked about her dread of it every time she made the trip. Didn't her beloved boss think of getting a ground-floor office? Or at least an office with fewer steps? I connected this oppression of my mother to the man with the mad daughter, who consorted with the worst kind of women in the world. I knew better than to criticize her boss to her, but in my mind I was angry for her dread, her labor, and I blamed him.

Next to the office where my mother worked was a dentist's office. We never saw the dentist go in or out and we never saw any patients. Occasionally, we smelled a chemical or heard the drill. Our feet were loud on the wooden floors, but when my mother opened the ground glass door with her boss's name painted on it in black lettering our feet were silent. The office was carpeted. It had no windows. You had to turn on, immediately on entering the door, the huge fluorescent lights. When you were there, you never had any idea of weather or time of day.

My mother had to do extra work on the weekends to make up for her irregular hours. Sometimes I would come with her. She would sit me in her boss's office, at her boss's desk. Only now does the idolatry of that strike me; at the time, I assumed she just wanted to give me space. I sat at the huge desk with the gold and onyx pens. I smelled the residual odor of cigars. I looked at the pictures of Jones Beach and Robert Moses. I read my books. I left the world of male progress for the pastel world, or the world of saints. I never aspired to grow up and sit at a desk like my mother's boss. But the space and the semi-darkness of the room allowed me to be happy.

All through my childhood, I had a recurrent dream in which my mother's boss undressed her and threw her, naked, out a window.

My only experience of happy play that involved another human being happened with my father.

Now things intrude which I, in my desire for orderli-ness, tried to keep out. I didn't want to speak about my father. I wanted to be talking about places. I wanted spaces emptied of people; I wanted to mention lights and shadows, eloquent emptiness, the melancholy of furni-ture, the loneliness of ceilings, the madness of mirrors, all those subjects coated, sluiced, in nutritive and fertilizing silence. Objects that speak for themselves.

But in wishing to inhabit only a world of innocent objects, am I going against the grain, against the family tradition and its legacy? We did not, as a family, care for objects and places. We did not, as a family, notice things. We would not have thought of traveling for scenery or architecture. We would not have thought of moving from one corner of a room to the other because the light was better. We did not believe in living by the eye. We told jokes, we made up stories, we sang songs. We prayed, together and separately, and in prayers, in the rise and fall of their periodic sentences, their invocations and ejacula-tions, in their seasonality and sense of occasion, we found what was, to us, a superior habitation of physical space.

It isn't only to honor the sense of us as a family that I have to speak about my father. I must speak about him if my subject is play. No one but him could create with me the made-up worlds that interested me.

To do this, we would meet in the living room. For me, the room was dominated by a closet with a cream-colored door and large, exaggerated wooden knob whose outer surface was flat rather than rounded. Inside this closet was housed recent history. The years after the war. The darkness immediately preceding my birth inhabited by adults who, not being parents, had the hard-edged importance of movie stars. The closet contained two things that were to be the emblems of the immediate and undomesticated past: A chrome-and-ebony cocktail shaker with six matching chrome manhattan glasses. A mother-of-pearl photograph album of my parents' wedding. And beside them, a box of Christmas tree ornaments, including a Neapolitan Christ child in a crib woven of things and filled with straw.

The closet was a prop room that turned our living room into a theater in which my father's and my play should be performed. With the manhattan glasses, filled with water, accompanied by Ritz crackers on a wooden tray, I was a priest, consecrating Hosts and putting them on my father's tongue. In the same religious vein, I put a doll's blanket around my head and took the infant Jesus out of his Christmas box (a daring gesture of unseasonal purloining). I put the baby Jesus on a hassock. My father knelt on one side of it, Saint Joseph, and I on the other, the adoring Virgin Mother. In another secular game, I wrapped my torso in a square of silk from my toy box and pretended to be Rosemary Clooney. My father was Bing Crosby (uncostumed) to whom I was married. As Rosemary, I grew blond, large, maternal. I sang to my singer husband, I cleansed domestic life of all its slowness, its repetitions, although I think the dialogue by which this was accomplished was fairly pedestrian. A large part of the pleasure of the act seemed to consist in my saying sentences whose importance was not in the information they conveyed but in the possibility they afforded of our using each other's stage names. "Hi, Bing." "Hi, Rosey." "How are the kids?" "The kids are fine. I'll just call Harry." (We had a son who, for some reason I cannot recall, was named Harry.) "Harry, come and have your breakfast."

Who is to blame for the fact that my father was the only one I liked playing with? Him, myself, or them? Those children who wanted to climb trees or play house. How could they compete with games of infinite glamour, infinite salvation?

Was it just my bad luck that there was nobody, not one child, who was interested in re-creating imaginary worlds of heroics and glamour? Was it my shame, in knowing myself so odd, that kept me apart from others of my kind? For it was certain that I knew myself in the wrong. Guilty of the crime of liking the wrong things. A vice I had to conceal, like a drug addict or a voyeur. Always I had to pretend to be more of a child than I was. At my baby-sitter's, I had to pretend to like cartoons, black-and-white histories of a farmer in long underwear, a couple of wiry hairs sprouting from his bald head. He would chase mice with his rifle or vacuum them up with his Hoover. I couldn't understand why anyone would find this a desirable spectacle, why anyone would want to watch *this* as opposed to what was on the other channel, Kate Smith, monumental, patriotic, singing "When the Moon Comes Over the Mountain," reassuring us that we were, and always would be, safe. How could I have said to a four, five or six year old: "I'll be the Virgin Mary. You can be Saint Joseph or the angel." "I'll be the priest, you be the communicant." "I'll be Rosemary Clooney, you be Bing Crosby. You mean you don't know the words to 'White Christmas'?"

And how could I bring any of my peers to the ramp behind the Howard Johnson's that was next to my baby-sitter's house where I would stand, holding out my imaginary long, wide, satin skirts. At the top of my lungs I would sing "Three Coins in the Fountain," the theme of a movie my father had taken me to see that I had loved. As I intoned, "Which one will the fountain bless? Which one will the fountain bless," I ran down the ramp, my arms outstretched—but to whom? I was right in believing that no child I knew could be interested in joining me in this endeavor.

I did try, sometimes, to play with other children, but the child I had closest access to was a doomed prospect. Ella was the daughter of our landlords. They were Italian. The father, Joe, worked on the docks, and the mother, Rina, who looked much older than she really was, so much so that I was shocked when she became pregnant, was endlessly, sadly kind, and when her children fought she urged them to "make nice." They had a couple of aunts and uncles who seemed to have walked over the ocean, straight from the old country: Aunt Providence, with huge calves that ended in tiny pointed slippers; Uncle Luigi, who sang all the time and took the children, just for fun, on pointless rides in his springless car. But I didn't like these rides; I was afraid of bumping my head, as Ella did once, on the car's tin roof.

The house we lived in belonged to them; they occupied the bottom floor. Unlike my family, they allotted places for their children to play in. The front porch was accessible to us in good weather, and in bad, the basement, cleaner, more fragrant, and less menacing than any I have ever known, was our domain. Occasionally, we would play store there. Or they would play and I would make satisfyingly regular towers of the canned formula Rina kept down there for her baby. Always there was the wonderful fragrance of Italian coffee permeating the apartment; it has continued to be, for me, the wholly benignant emblem of domestic order. Sometimes Joe brought burlap sacks full of raw pistachios back from the docks; and he would roast them and invite us down for a feast. Hot, with a dark outer skin and an inner flesh of green that was one of the pastels of my good world, they would release their strong, exciting, nourishing flavor when we bit down on them, our lips a little sore from the salt Joe coated them in. We would have as many as we wanted; there was no end to what filled that burlap sack.

I don't like myself for the way I treated Ella. Ella was a perfectly nice girl. That she had no imagination, that she was prone to sties and asthma, that she pronounced egg "eyg," and leg "layg," that she was interested in coloring books and concentrated on staying in the lines, that she could not sing and could not read—all that was my bad luck and unrelated to her virtue. She is the occasion for my only memories of childhood violence. Both were concerned with language.

An only child, I never had the opportunity to hit another human being. To have hit my parents would have been as incomprehensible as hitting a cloud or a tree. But one day, Ella and I settled on a game that was acceptable to us. We were playing bride. We were both brides, and had imaginary grooms. We sang the bridal march for ourselves. But Ella sang—or did whatever she did with her tuneless voice—the song differently from me. I sang it, "Here comes the bride, all dressed in white, here comes the bridegroom right by her side." Ella insisted on rendering the words, "Here comes the bride, all dressed in white, marching to the altar all dressed in white." At first, I calmly tried to point out her mistake. She was resistant. I told her that it didn't make any sense to say that a bride was marching, marching was for parades, and a walk down the aisle was nothing like a parade. Her intransigence made me lose my humanity. I pushed her to the floor and knelt on her chest, pulling her hair until she would admit her error. She refused. We had to be separated by her mother, who was shocked at the glimpse of rage in a child she'd assumed to be well behaved and trustworthy. Another time, I hit her head against the wall for saying "It's so fun." I told her she could say "It's so much fun" or

"It's so funny," but not "It's so fun." Again, she mutely refused to admit the rightness of my position. I had to hurt her.

Ella's older sister was even worse for me. She horrified me. She was an overlarge girl with premature hair on her legs and forearms. Somehow she knew that I had seen my father naked, and she pressed me, with a furtive desperation, to describe the male body. "Is it like a carrot," she asked. "No, I don't know," I answered in a panic, only wanting to be far away from her so I could breathe clean air.

One year a family with children moved next door. The girl's name was Leonie, and I was delighted by its foreign sound, but puzzled because Leonie, which ended in an "e" sound, was not a nickname for anything, not an intimate form of the formal Leon. I remember sitting on a stepladder in her garage. I remember a boy named Robert Guthrie sitting on a step below me. I remember thinking his neck was beautiful, and kissing it. He ran away, appalled, and I never saw him again. I think I was five years old.

In the house behind us a boy lived with his slattern mother. I think he was feebleminded. On him I practiced the torturer's all-too-easy art, and I understood the impulse of the torturer; the relief, having been humiliated, of humiliation. Over the hedge I heard the mother say through her missing teeth, "Christopher, time for your noo-nap." Elated at this slender proof of my superiority, I cried out at the top of my voice, "Noo, nap, noo, nap, Christopher it's time to take your noo-nap." I saw his abashed, shamed face, and I knew myself loathsome. I hid myself indoors for the rest of the day. I never allowed myself to look at Christopher or his mother again; I ran or hid if I saw them, and from that day to this, I have known the bad news of my nature.

I suppose I could, if there had been one around, have found a way to play with a certain kind of little girl, because in a rare instance of conventionality, I was fond of dolls. Not dolls that embodied visions of a pastel world, a world of ruffles and of prettiness. I liked dolls that looked like babies. I liked the reenactment of the scut work of motherhood. I liked washing their naked bodies, scrubbing their hair or their naked skulls. I liked dressing and undressing them. Some of them had hard heads. I remember a hurt when, bending down to serve my silent baby, I cracked skulls with her (an adumbration of filial betrayal or maternal pain?). Some of the dolls had distressingly squishy bodies, friable rubber flesh that would split or crack, revealing woolly innards that made them hateful and worthy of condemnation and rejection. Their insubstantial wrists, bent once too often, strained and stretched and revealed potential horrors, like a harbor in spring when the hard surface of the ice recedes and gradually reveals things better left unseen.

I remember doing something with a doll that now seems very strange but struck me at the time as a simple exploration. A doll that I wasn't very fond of was suffering the disease of split skin. Inside the skin were small rubber trapezoids, green and red, the size of lentils or split peas. I must have made the association, and I decided to rip the skin apart, put the rubber peas into a pan of water and pretend to cook them. My mother discovered me doing this, and came at me with a fury I couldn't really understand. "What are you doing?" she shouted, her eyes wild, gripping my shoulders in a way that she must have known would cause pain. "Cooking Suzy's insides," I said. She emptied the potful into the sink and said she couldn't stand the sight of me.

Was she so disturbed because she saw, beneath the smooth skin of the child, the bloody appetite of the cannibal? I went into my room (her room), covered by a sense of shame, obscure because I couldn't really trace its roots. Later she said to me, "I hate anything destructive," and the words spun and shimmered with a force and darkness I found exhilarating, valuable in itself, although I knew it must be hidden, forever. I was terrified and strengthened, knowing what was inside me, what could come out if the strain caused the outer surface to become friable, like the skin of my dolls, whose failure to remain intact required punishment.

There was a doll I dreamed of, the idea for which came from a book my father brought home from the city. The book had a green shiny cover and its title was in raspberry-colored lettering: *The Surprise Doll*. The girl in the story was named Sally. I never knew anyone named Sally, but it seemed like the perfect name for the kind of happy girl that I would never be. Sally was blond. She wore red overalls and a yellow shirt, her father had a job which required a lot of travel. From every place he visited, or rather went for his work (we were assured his travel wasn't done for pleasure), he brought her a doll representative of the place. She named each of the dolls. There was Fifi from France, Hilda from Germany, Inge from Sweden, Caterina from Italy, Lola from Spain, Le-Ying from Hong Kong, Misoko from Japan. There were Eskimo dolls and Indian dolls, whose civilization was understood to be too uncomplicated to bestow names. But finally, on one trip whose destination was unclear, the father brought home a doll that looked exactly like Sally. She had Sally's blond hair, blue eyes, button nose. She wore red overalls and a yellow shirt. Sally held in her hands a miniature of herself; she looked in the eyes of a double.

I also played for many hours with paper dolls, what we called cutouts. They were cardboard replicas of movie stars and the ones that I liked best were blond and girl-ish—June Allyson, Jane Powell. Emanating from them was a sense of their incompleteness without the partnership of men, as if they were always standing, their arms at their sides, waiting, or else with their arms open, expecting to be chosen, to be danced with, to be carried off. I would make these cardboard figures walk, talk to each other. I would give them an ordinary life. Mostly, I would change and rechange their clothes: they were suited and hatted women of the world, or playful sun worshipers in polka-dotted bathing suits; most thrillingly, they were, finally, dressed in elaborate ball gowns. When I was finished play-ing with them, I'd undress them and put them in my toy box, on their way to nowhere but chaste dreams.

*   *   *

The summer after my father died, I was sent away. I was sent as an exile. The worst kind of exile, a person banished because someone with power believes it is being done for the victim's own good. But actually, I was banished because I bore a disease by which the virtuous people of the republic felt in danger of being contaminated. I suffered the disease of excessive and obsessive mourning.

My father had died in February. I was numbed by pain, and I entered a world of darkness. A world in which, it occurs to me now, there was no possibility of play. The theater that was our living room was closed to me forever. We had moved away. All our things had been packed.

I didn't think of asking what had happened to my toys. Why the circus-colored box didn't travel with me, with my clothes, with my schoolbooks and my special blanket. Two of my dolls traveled with me, the toughies, portable and durable, not taking up too much space. The baby mannequin that my father had wheedled from a friend who owned a children's store, the china doll I never quite knew what to do with but liked the idea of— they were off somewhere. Somewhere. This is what I wish to speculate on now, not the idea of the crudity, the cruelty of my elders, nor the spectacle of my own deprivation. I simply wonder where in the world those things went. Were they given to another child, a poor child, a foreign child, a refugee from tyranny? Were they simply put in the garbage? Were they given, not to the Salvation Army (we were Catholics, we patronized our own charities) but to the Society of Saint Vincent de Paul? Were they sent to a children's hospital to give succor to the dying? Whoever got my old toys could not have been among the fortunate.

Misunderstanding my transformation into a mourner or misjudging what might be the proper cure, my mother's brothers and sisters, that is to say my aunts and uncles, thought of sending me to a camp the summer after my father's death, to a place where I could play outside in the fresh air, like an ordinary, or an ordinarily deprived child.

The name of the place I went to was Lake Paradox. Only now do I wonder about the source of that name. Was it a mistake or a joke? Did some immigrant think he was naming it after a synonym for heaven? Or was it a jaded logician thinking he would take a busman's holiday?

My uncles and aunts and their spouses bought a property on Lake Paradox, near Schroon Lake, in the Adirondacks. It was an estate with three houses on it, and the houses all had names. The Beta, the Traveller, and the Casa Mia. I don't know why the definite article was used for all three.

My aunts and uncles decided they would run a boys' camp there. They spent many years rescuing the estate from dereliction, and in 1956, the year before my father's death, it was ready. There were a series of dormitories built (none of the big houses housed campers), and in the Traveller was the kitchen where my grandmother, then in her seventies, did all the cooking for the campers and the dining room where they all ate. The camp was not a success. At its highest point, there were only twelve paying campers. The rest were cousins, and, after my father's death, I was included, though I was the only girl, neither a tomboy nor athletic. I can't imagine why anyone thought I might be happy there.

And no one seemed to go out of their way to find anything for me to do. I was allowed to bring my dog with me, so I wandered the property, thrilled by my discovery of a shrine to Saint Anthony over a perpetually cold spring, where beer and wine were chilled. I slept in a bed with my grandmother. We slept alone in the large house, and she kept a baseball bat by the bed against intruders. She woke early, to make breakfast for everyone: French toast, Wheatena, pancakes on Saturday, but only after Mass. I woke after her, and was left to myself. I was wretchedly lonely, and I cried a lot. My aunt, who was the camp nurse, got me a postcard with the gap-toothed face of *Mad* magazine's Alfred E. Neuman that said "Keep Smiling." She suggested I hang it above my bed.

It was a boys' camp, and so everything was geared for boys. Including, of course, the books in the tiny library. It was here that I had my first experience of reading a book I didn't like: an abridged version of *The Last of the Mohicans.* I could find no foothold in this book, no place to lay my head. And books had always been my refuge, my sanctuary. But this book was rejecting me, reminding me that it was possible even in this land of safety to be alien.

I associate this sense of alienation with the claylike smell of the lavatory, which seemed to me to indicate a waste product coming from a body utterly unlike my own, a male body, human but inhuman, colorless, and close to death. It was connected to the rust stain underneath the faucet in the bathroom and the fact that, most of the time, the water was not hot, and so I was encouraged to bathe in the lake, given a sliver of soap and a thin towel, told to wash "inside my bathing suit," so that I never, in those months, felt myself to be clean.

One of the few things I enjoyed was going into the house called the Casa Mia, because there was a huge fireplace made of fieldstone, and a screened-in porch that smelled of cedar. But the greatest appeal of that place was a stash of old magazines, and it was there I found the image of the woman who hypnotized me. Or no, not one woman, a series of them, more or less alike, but importantly, not exactly interchangeable.

In the morning I would make my way to the Casa Mia, to the magazines. I think they were *Good Housekeeping*. On the back cover, month after month, in an oval surround, was a picture of the Breck Girl. She wore pearls. She had blond or light brown hair, a pageboy, white skin, thin lips, eyes of no color that might attract attention. A face with no emotional register, no hint of anger or alarm, or for that matter joy or exultation. A face that was a vehicle for neither thought nor words. A face that effaced the idea of the importance of language. And those pearls! I stared. I shuffled the months: September, October, February, June. I fixed on the feathery eyebrows, the pink bow lips. I imagined no narrative for these faces, simply, as I had in my father's office, an atmosphere. A face surrounded by emptiness, a face emanating from pure light. This, it seemed to me, was the desirable estate of women. No woman I had ever seen was anything like this. These women were impossible, therefore invaluable. This is how I spent my mornings, until I joined the noisy jostling boys for lunch, then afternoon sports, at which I miserably failed.

I failed at basketball, I failed at tennis. I failed at nature study. I exasperated my aunt by saying I saw the birds she was pointing out when she knew that I didn't. I thought the crafts were ridiculous, and my other aunt, who supervised the crafts, felt punitive when she correctly interpreted my contempt.

After three weeks of enduring the spectacle of my multiple failures, everyone seemed to agree to leave me alone. I was no longer watched, probably because the sight of me was distasteful, or perhaps painful to them. It was a great relief to be invisible, although I understood that the adult world at large had joined me in giving up forever on the idea of my being a child. But I was free to do the things I really liked. I no longer had to pretend to play. Each morning I took my books up the hill to the Casa Mia, where I could sit alone in front of the cold, useless fireplace. Beside me, I spread out my saints' lives and my fairy tales and my wrinkled copies of *Good Housekeeping*. All day, I read and looked at pictures. All day, my head was filled with thoughts of lovely women, virtuous, heroic, or women whose lives had neither story nor event, all of them rescued, at the last possible moment, by a man who loved them, who would save them from their dangers and their fates.

THE COUNTRY
NEXT DOOR

OURS WAS A house of female habitation, and the house next door was not. Theirs was painted light blue: the trim around the windows and the doors was forest green. The house was an island in a river of two driveways, one on either side of it, one blacktopped, one cement. What went on in the driveways was important, and things did go on there, because there were so many vehicles of different types; cars, of course, but also motorcycles and a pickup truck.

As a young child, I had no inclination to approach the house. There was no need to. Not that there was no communication between houses; simply I wasn't part of it. My grandmother and Lina, the woman of the house next door, talked with the rushed, vexed precision of master housewives; they did not complain, but they enumerated all their tasks. If they'd been men, work*men,* that is, perhaps they would have laid their tools out side by side and talked about building a house, or a road. If they'd been workmen, they'd have worked alongside each other, probably silently, possibly breaking into song occasionally or telling jokes. But Lina and my grandmother would meet only for moments over the fence as they hung laundry; they might shout things to each other as they dug or harvested their gardens. Then they would separate. They were, neither of them, the kind of women who would join up in one of their kitchens for coffee. Perhaps because, although my grandmother was forty years older, they had one important thing in common: they had both been domestic servants.

When I think of my grandmother and Lina, when I think of anything associated with the house next door, the tasks of categorization and making distinctions, of determining the cause of things, seems impossible, a foolish project and a wasteful one. It is possible to say and say correctly that both Lina and my grandmother were domestic servants. But having said that, what good have I done? Yes, they were both domestic servants, they were paid by employers to oversee the most intimate workings of their bodies, they fed their employers, they removed the traces of their filth, they repaired assaults on order and beauty. They allowed those who gave them wages to pretend that they survived as animals without effort. They were at others' beck and call.

But, having named the similarities, who is to say whether they are more important than the differences? For Lina and my grandmother were very different people who led very different lives, so, having said that they'd both been domestic servants, what is there to say that could be any kind of explanation for everything that followed? Similarly, of what help is it to know, of Lina's daughter and myself, that we slept every night no more than fifty yards from each other, in the same years of the world's history, and that for some years we saw each other every morning of our lives?

But why am I speaking about women when my subject is the house next door, a house whose purpose was to shelter or serve men, to satisfy them, to give them a place to go. Because it was as obvious to me then as it is now that Lina and her body's life were central to the house and set a sort of tone from which reverberations followed, just as my grandmother's did for ours.

Does history create certain body types or do certain body types simply come into their own in some periods of history? What happens to the other types? Do they go on living their lives, the owners of these bodies, consigned to partial invisibility, unphotographed, unmarried, silent, too, because unsung? There was a place for my grandmother's body at the end of the last century; the times called for long-waisted, full-bosomed, wide-shouldered women, with limbs like the trunks of vigorous trees in a forest open, as yet, to no man's ax.

My grandmother never changed the style of her hair. It was pinned, simply, to the top of her head through immigration, life in a strange country, marriage, childbirth, matriarchy. So remarkable were the times when I saw her with her hair down that I remember them distinctly. Times when she was ill, near to death, and her hair was spread out around her on her pillow like a sign from another age, a sign of surrender, which had she not been near death, she would have forbidden.

The other times I saw her with her hair down were inexplicably celebratory. They happened when she washed her hair, in summer, in the backyard. Why did my grandmother insist on such publicness? Why did she make such a performance of her grooming? It happened only once a year, this performance. Is it possible that she washed her hair only once a year? It was very thin and I knew her only as an old woman. My grandmother's hair was always the color of beaten silver; in the sun it shone.

But once a year she took it down, and she insisted that whatever children were around participate or witness. Before we arrived from wherever it was that we had been, she'd set out a bench and on it a battered tin basin filled with water, a blue towel, a white comb, a white pitcher, a bottle of Halo shampoo. Then while we stood—honored, deferential, terrified—she took the bone pins from her hair. She allowed her hair to fall out of its bun—she didn't move to undo it. There was a moment of suspense between our glimpse of her hair, collected in a knob at the top of her skull, and its trans-formation into its witchlike decline, lifeless and energy-less, suggesting nothing beautiful, no hope.

She draped the blue towel around her shoulders. She filled the pitcher from the basin; the spillage seeped into the grass. She held the pitcher over her head and bent her head back; her hair hung behind her skull like a thin flag. With her hair wet, the bones of her cheeks and the sharp-ness of her nose made her seem of the party of death. She poured shampoo into her hand and lathered her head. A lathered head turned her comic, girlish. We might, we speculated, be allowed to laugh. She massaged her scalp, but not for long, not long at all considering how rare these shampoos were. She poured another pitcherful of water from the basin and then rinsed her soapy hair. She did this twice, then she squeezed her hair in the towel that had been on her shoulders. She combed her hair with her wide-toothed white comb. Then she leaned back, closed her eyes, and enjoyed the sunshine. All this time we children stood and watched. We didn't move until our grandmother stood up and brought her things into the kitchen.

Lina's hair was tightly curled. Whenever I hear the line from Shakespeare's sonnet, "If hair be wires, black wires grow on her head," I think of Lina's hair. Each Saturday she had it done at the beauty parlor. I know that because every week she came back with pastries she'd got as a bargain from the bakery next door to the beautician's. Her hair appointment was four o'clock; each week she'd finish at 5:30. The bakery closed at six, and was willing to sell its leftovers cheap in preparation for its big day: Sunday, when people loaded up on rolls and coffee cakes on their way home from church. Lina left a rye bread and four danishes—one for each of us, my grandmother, my aunt, my mother, and myself. We never offered to pay: it was as if, all of us lacking the protection of a man, there'd be no question of our paying. We didn't eat in front of her. She left the white bag on the kitchen table; within seconds she was out the door.

Her hair was at its stiffest on these Saturday visits; it only just missed being clownish. A controlled athleticism emanated from her hair as it did from the rest of her body. Unlike the women in my house, she had no breasts or hips. You would say she was boyish, but nothing about her suggested the playful, the carefree, or the unplanned. So she wasn't boyish. Something soldierly perhaps: a young cadet. She was so tall that she often wore flat shoes. I think of her penny loafers and her ankle bracelet visible beneath her stockings.

I never saw her cook. I saw her often with her vacuum cleaner. She was devoted to cleanliness, but she was much more dependent on appliances and bottled chemicals than my grandmother.

The day she had wall-to-wall carpeting installed was a great event. It was perfectly smooth, emerald or grass colored, and it felt bouncy to the feet. You felt the bounce in the soles of your feet because Lina made everyone take their shoes off on the side porch. In our circle, this was unheard of: pretentious, pseudo-Japanese, a remarkable request for a woman married to Larry Schneider, much more remarkable that it would be obeyed.

Marrying Larry Schneider had got Lina out of domestic service.

Of Lina's life before she came to Queens I have little idea. Only the mention of a farm, parents who did not speak English. An abashed sister who appeared once or twice in my memory, looking nothing like Lina, from another life, another country, her hair perhaps not naturally different from Lina's, the same dry kinks, but bound up in a net. More shocking to a fashion-conscious child (myself) she wore high heels with white socks. How did Lina get herself out from the house that produced this sister, the house that produced her, into her first job in the house of Ted and Nita Hall? How did they hire her? How did she make herself available for hire?

Like Lina's, the story of Nita Hall has its elements of class mobility. My mother had gone to school with her, but in school she was Winnie Mitchell. Her full name was Juanita. What Spanish dream—Juanita, Señorita—had led her parents, ordinary native-born Americans, to such an exotic naming of their daughter? But in the early twenties, "Winnie" better suited the girl she wanted to be, the coed with cloche hat and raccoon coat. "She always had looks, she had something, all right; the boys were nuts about her," my mother said with the rushed awe of the never buried teenage girl. At eighteen, Winnie married someone a bit above her station. Quite a bit. Joe Hall, a lawyer, twenty-one, a college man. He prospered; they had, instead of children, a series of increasingly grander houses. She transformed herself from a coed to a femme fatale, from cuddlesome to continental. She wore her hair pulled back, held with a tortoiseshell barrette. And she hired Lina, with whom she allowed herself to become friends. So that, long after Nita had stopped being her employer, long after Lina left her to marry Larry Schneider, the two women similar in body type (was this their link: looking at each other did they experience the mirror-gazer's thrill?) continued to visit and to mark each other's birthdays and anniversaries with gifts that were sometimes small, sometimes large.

We all convinced ourselves that Larry Schneider was secretly generous, secretly adoring, because otherwise there was no reason for the match. Lina was fastidious. Not only her house, but her clothing was fanatically well ordered. Her fingernails were perfectly polished, she was never without lipstick, and she never varied the cultivated artificiality of her eyebrows: two thin, penciled lines that required an excision of what had been given her by nature. She was never unkempt, never sweaty or ill-dressed, and all this in the midst of a terrific, never-ending labor. The labor of a housewife.

Except that, as I said, I never saw her cook. In this she was different from my grandmother, whose cooking was legendary (it was spoken about outside her presence, it was almost the first thing said about her). I never heard Lina or anyone around her speak of food and I never smelled cooking in her house. Our house was permeated by delicious smells. My grandmother's cooking was a product of history. She was Irish, but she became an excellent Italian cook for the same reasons that she learned the Italian language: she wanted to protect herself from her husband's relations who were appalled by his marrying an Irish girl, a foreigner. She was exactly right in her intuitions; she earned the respect, the awe of her new relatives. There was, to them, something witchlike, in the sense of the desirably supernatural, in this large, fair Irish girl who could cook like them and speak their language. Who could talk to the Yankees and then to them. It meant they all had a new place in America, and they were safer because of it.

My grandmother always cooked the large quantities of the farmwife; like Lina, she had begun life on a farm. Then she had nine children, a good number for a farmer. She boasted of how she'd satisfied the unending appetites of her four sons. She never spoke of cooking for her daughters, nor would she have bragged about their eating. Lina had three sons, but she never mentioned feeding them, only the messes that they made. Of her daughter, she rarely spoke at all.

I remember an incident involving food and Lina's two younger sons. Tommy and Robbie crossed the border into our yard; they had never done that before. In all the years I lived next door to them, I never went near them; the gulf between us seemed unbridgeable, the worlds we inhabited had no overlap. They played ball and fought and shouted. They were dirty, they climbed fences, they dug in the ground for nothing, for fool's gold or worms. I read lives of the saints and fairy tales and dreamed of learning foreign languages, particularly French. I stayed out of their way.

Why, one day, did they decide they wanted to torment me? It was a day in the fall, November, the sky was pewter colored and the earth had hardened to a neutral gray and brown. I was in the backyard, doing nothing. I can't imagine what I might have been doing there. Whatever I was doing, it had nothing to do with Lina's sons. Perhaps they thought it did. Perhaps they thought that I was spying. But on what? Their football game? Their throwing their coats on the dry lawn? I think there was no reason but bored malice for the thing they did.

In my grandmother's garden, which was separated from the backyard where I stood by a large evil-looking, stone-colored garage, there were the remains of rhubarb plants. Unplucked, they'd grown gigantic; their stalks were ruby colored, the leaves the size of palm fronds that could roof a Caribbean hut.

The boys must have picked the rhubarb silently, because they were suddenly behind me. Tommy, the younger one, knocked me on my back without a word. He pinned me by the shoulders. Robbie knelt on my thighs. It was he who shoved the rhubarb into my mouth. "Eat it," he said. "Eat it all."

I knew I had no choice. The rhubarb was the texture of celery, only stringier, and terribly bitter. Its redness made me think of blood and I felt my stomach fill with blood that rose up to my mouth. But I said to myself, Pretend it's celery. Pretend nothing is happening, only that you're eating celery. I was sure if I opened my mouth to scream, blood would come pouring from it. I didn't scream, and they were silent. Our mutual silence, the hardness and brownness of the ground, created underneath my terror a layer that suggested endless patience, even perhaps leisure; they were in no rush, and there was nowhere I could go. Then suddenly they grew bored. Still silent, they let me up and ran away. I wouldn't have dreamed of telling anyone. I was ashamed, I think, of being such a helpless object of malignity, and I knew I wasn't really hurt. I knew that it was possible to say nothing had happened.

Having spoken—though I didn't speak about it when it happened—about something related to their superior strength, not to say capacity for violence, I should talk about the actual bodies of the males next door.

I can't imagine what it must have been like for Lina to allow herself to be approached by someone having Larry's body. I use the word *having* deliberately, but perhaps I use it wrongly. I can't help it though. I can't think about it in a better way, because Larry's physical presence in the world was so odd. He had a body, but very little of it was visible. He was always in mechanic's overalls.

Can that be possible that he was never seen in anything but overalls? That no social occasion, feast or celebration, wedding, funeral, would have called up in him the sense of obligation to dress in anything but the emblems of his work? And, bear in mind, his work was filthy. Lina made him go right to the basement the minute he came home. She told us this. None of us ever saw the sink where he was made to scrub his hands, the shower where he was made to cleanse himself, the robe and slippers that he wore upstairs into the living quarters. None of us ever saw him, if he happened to go over in the evenings to borrow something, if the phone was broken, if my grandmother was sending Lina vegetables.

There were no vegetables in Lina's garden, only severe, military-looking flowers, primary colors, upright and unyielding and alert.

You must understand Larry's nearly complete invisibility, so sharply different from Lina's steady and unchallengeable insistence upon being seen. He didn't have the invisibility of a ghost, there was nothing light about him; it was the invisibility of a burrowing animal, you knew he was somewhere doing something, but it went on in darkness. And like an animal that burrowed, he appeared, when he was visible, to have no face.

I remember his having a mouth, a cartoonlike something that spread and revealed teeth that were only blunt, as if there were no incisors. Instruments of grinding not of biting. With these teeth a laughing child could be ground up. Anything could. He was balding, so the half-dome of his skull was another featureless plane, repeating his face. It was very possible he had no eyes, or that they were covered with skin, like a mole or a lizard. He moved heavily; his forearms were unusually short.

And what about the other male bodies in the house? Because, it is important to remember, this is an important way of knowing Lina, an important way she knew herself: she was the mother of three sons.

The first was named Carl, after Larry's father who lived two streets away, truly invisible, and was said never to go out. Lina cooked food for him but it was brought by Larry. No one but Larry was allowed to go into his house.

Lina's son Carl was oversize, a kind of giant, though he was not grotesque, just monumental. I remember seeing his empty boots near the side door where all the shoes were kept. They frightened me and thrilled me; they were a glimpse into a world, crude, powerful, potentially overwhelming, that nothing about living in our house had prepared me for.

Carl drove a motorcycle: it roared up the block destroying the idea of all domestic comfort or domestic peace. He had dirty blond hair that always seemed literally dirty. He wore it like James Dean and I never saw him in anything but black pants, a white T-shirt, and a black motorcycle jacket. But I didn't see too much because I was afraid to look at him. His face was like a naked phallus and it felt unseemly to be casting my eyes on its rawness, its intrusions into the world.

I think, being so tall for a woman, Lina liked standing beside her giant son. At nineteen, he married a woman in her forties, older than his mother, plainer, coarser, and less glamorous. She rode on the back of his motorcycle. Lina told my grandmother they had terrible fights, that she threw things at him—glasses, bottles—when she'd been drinking. Sometimes at two or three in the morning Carl would roar up the driveway on his motorbike, alone, and bang on the door for his mother to let him in.

The two younger boys, my tormenters, were eight and six years younger than Carl and didn't share his large proportions. Tommy had thick glasses, thin fingers, and the thin, flaxen hair of an ill-nourished orphan. Robbie had his mother's sharp looks; he had a sidelong, sharky smile that always made you feel he had a secret that would do you harm. He was deft with his hands and quick with his feet. He was the street champion at touch football. He almost never spoke.

It never seemed that Lina had much interest in her younger sons. They often seemed to be at large; they roamed the neighborhood, and even after dark they were in other people's yards. It was as if her strength for being an attentive mother to a son had been worn out, absorbed, like certain vitamins, by the experience of having carried in her body her huge, oldest son.

When Robbie was eight, Lina had another baby. This time a girl.

I don't know what the pacing of Lina's reproductive life meant. One son, then eight years later, another, followed two years later by another one. Then another eight-year gap until she got what clearly she had always wanted: a daughter. But was it what she'd always wanted? Weren't sons enough? I can't think, from the way that she would stand beside him, that Carl was not enough for her. Perhaps it was only the middle two she didn't want. Perhaps it was because of that they were so silent, so silent and so punishing. But perhaps they were punishing only that one time, only to me.

Lina named her daughter Cindi. It was the first time any of us in the house next door had ever heard of a name ending in *i*. And not a nickname either. A name that someone would be christened with, or by. Of course it was the Lutheran church, not ours, the Catholic. Larry was Lutheran, but Lina was Polish and must have been born Catholic. Why had his religious choice held sway, since nothing else connected with him had? It was impossible to imagine that Larry could have had a religious life. But who knows what demands might have been placed on Lina in return for her having been freed from the bondage of domestic servitude? Who knows what threats were placed on her by Larry or his reclusive father? Or was there a mother at the time of the wedding? No one had ever heard of her.

Cindi. The name revealed the truth of Lina's wishes: she wanted a doll, a lively mannequin. How she dressed her girl child, in the tenderest beribboned dresses, smocking and embroidery, organdy and ruffles! Bought from Best & Co. in Garden City: Larry could afford it, he was making a fortune on his new specialty, foreign cars. As the fifties rolled to their conformist end, foreign cars were still rare enough to make their servicing valuable and profitable.

None of the lovely dresses did what Lina dreamed. Cindi was dull and lumpish; her nose ran constantly; she cried for nothing. She fell often on the soft green carpet, so, although she had to clumsily reconstruct herself, she was never bruised. I wonder how long it was before Lina stopped looking on her daughter with her eye of favor. Cindi was fond of animals, and by the time she was five she had her own menagerie of rodents in a series of cages in the basement, near the sink and shower where her father was made to wash before he was allowed upstairs.

How did Lina, who seemingly felt so little for her, allow her to find her real love, horses? Cindi was a horsey girl, but there was nothing decorative about her on a saddle. She sat her horse like a farmer. The heritage that Lina had come down the Hudson to escape implanted itself firmly in her daughter's thick limbs. Cindi learned to ride English, then to jump. But even in her costly helmet, jodhpurs, boots, she could only enact the role of the clumsily dressed-up peasant. She won ribbon after ribbon. Lina didn't seem pleased or proud, although she drove Cindi to every show, and displayed all her trophies and ribbons in a special case.

I wonder what my grandmother's sickness and death had to do with what happened in the house next door.

My grandmother was a tower, a mountain, an overhanging cliff in whatever landscape she appeared. She was the great mother to the literally motherless, and to a squadron of self-defined orphans. She had nine children of her own; none of them died in childbirth, although three were later stricken by polio. Three crippled children, and she attended to them, took them for treatments, got them operations, exercised their withered limbs, and, above all, did not allow them, any of them, none of the three of them, a moment of self-pity. In addition to her own nine, she took into her family the children of afflicted mothers: once for two years the daughter of a friend of my grandmother's, whose mother had been crippled with arthritis; for another year, the daughter of a woman who'd gone to a TB sanitarium; then for several years, the children of my grandfather's sister, who were being taken away from their mother on account of her having left her husband to move in with another man. What happened to these children after the brief periods they stayed in my grandmother's house? They came back as adults, grateful, adoring. What could they do for my grandmother to show their gratitude, their veneration? Nothing. It was impossible to think of anything to do for my grandmother. She seemed to everyone a person of no desires and no needs.

And then one day she simply collapsed. She was eighty-two. She fell onto the floor, succumbing to a hemorrhage. Her daughters were at work; I was at school. She telephoned Lina. It was Lina who took her to the hospital, and only from there did she phone my mother and my aunt. Everyone pretended to be grateful to her, but it was a family that made no real place—though they were capable of simulating a false one, or perhaps an anteroom, a vestibule—for strangers.

They resented Lina but they relied on her. I was a child. She was strong and young and home all day. From that time on, the time of my grandmother's first illness, I adored her. She was truly reliable, as I had been told men were supposed to be.

The doctor said there was no hope for my grandmother. Her stomach cancer was advanced. She was sent home to die.

Like everything else she'd done, her dying was accomplished stubbornly and thoroughly. I'd never seen her rush, and she would certainly not rush her dying.

My tall, strong grandmother took up her drawn-out dying. She lost everything; speech first, and then mobility and mind. Her bedroom became a sickroom; her children became her nurses. We did hire a nurse, someone from the parish, whom my grandmother accused of stealing. We thought it was her mind wandering. We thought it was a dying woman's ravings, but later we found out the nurse was a kleptomaniac and that her husband had to go back to the family of every dying person she had cared for and return the money and the objects she had stolen while she was—and she genuinely was—easing the drawn-out death. No one ever let on about her stealing, because she'd been so much help. The families looked back on her times with them and believed they couldn't have done it without her. And they were right. She was not afraid to be near death. Besides, she was a member of the parish and to tell her shame would have brought shame, somehow, upon the parish as a whole.

I was thirteen the year of my grandmother's dying. During that year I bought my first bra. My mother bought it with me, wearily: she was exhausted with the care of her mother, and acknowledging my developing body was one more task she wished she could avoid. That year, too, when I was sitting in the backyard in the wettish grass, one day in April, my period came for the first time. My mother and I had been prepared; I'd read a pamphlet called *Growing Up and Liking It*; I had a box of sanitary napkins—Teenage by Modess—in an orange-and-white-flowered wrapper. I told my mother; she asked if I had any questions. I had none. I couldn't think of what a possible question might be.

*   *   *

After Easter dinner that year, Lina invited me for a cup of tea. It was a very strange thing for her to do; as I said, we never went to her house to eat and I never thought of her as doing something so relaxed as drinking tea. I was afraid that I'd done something wrong, and although my conscience was clear, I was used to being surprised by something being thought of as a misdeed or a sign of pride. I was ready for a reproach whose source I couldn't trace.

Lina looked at me with her black eyes.

"Have you ever worn high heels?"

"No."

"Do you want to?"

"Someday."

"When?"

"I don't know. I haven't thought about it."

"You should think about it. I hate girls who walk badly in high heels. They look like drunks. It marks them, it always marks them. I want to show you how to walk right in heels. I want you to practice with me."

I was intensely grateful. Someone, it seemed, had noticed I was getting older.

She took me upstairs into her closet. Her shoes were stored in hanging plastic bags; a separate compartment for each pair of shoes. In the wide mouth of each shoe was a contraption that looked like a wooden tongue with a handle. Shoe trees, I told myself. Though, because my mother and my aunt had only one pair of specially made built-up shoes, and because my grandmother owned only one pair of dress shoes and one for work, I'd never seen such a thing before.

"We'll start with these. They're high but not too thin."

She put on my feet a pair of shoes that must have been twenty years old. Shoes from the war, from the early forties. They were navy blue with white piping around the arch. Open toes. She had me practice walking on the carpet, then on wood, back and forth in front of her, then back and forth again, then up and down the stairs. I don't think she offered any advice. Only one comment: "You need practice."

It was two years later that I got my first pair of high heels, black patent leather, pointy-toed spikes. I didn't teeter, and I never turned my ankle, as some of my friends did.

My grandmother had been dead six months when what my mother referred to as "all that business" started happening next door.

It was New Year's Eve. My mother and I were somber in our celebrations. We were alone, and although we wouldn't have thought of going to bed before midnight, we didn't have very good ideas about how to go about a celebration. I was too young to be given more than a sip of champagne; my mother preferred her habitual vermouth to any other drink. Under my grandmother's peasant rule, we weren't a family who went in for snacks. I don't think that in all the years I lived with my mother we ever bought a bag of potato chips.

We watched Guy Lombardo on the television; we sang "Auld Lang Syne" with him and his Royal Canadians, we stood at the front door and banged pots with wooden spoons like the other neighbors.

Except next door. Next door there were very different goings-on. Couples appeared, arm in arm, tipsy on the street, their party hats askew on their party-coiffed heads. They had real noisemakers, they shouted "Happy New Year" onto the street long after the other neighbors had fallen asleep in the darkness.

It was in sleep that I heard what I've called the event. A man's voice, startlingly loud in the dead January night, was crying out. It was a kind of sleepy keening, clearly drunken, in its repetitiveness and the complete forgetfulness of the range of possibly appropriate tones, in its pained yet mocking self-absorption. Over and over the voice cried out, "Good night Lina, good night Lina, good night Lina, good night." Then the sound disappeared; it had been coming from the open window of a car that was driving down the street and at some point was too far away for its passenger's signals to be heard.

The next morning, Lina came in with rolls.

"That was something last night. Poor Jack—I hope he didn't wake you."

Lina had a habit of assuming we knew all her friends although, except for Nita, we knew none of them.

"You can hardly believe it. He's the quietest guy in the world. I don't know what got into him. I guess you could say one too many."

It was not the sort of thing you could say much in

reply to, and there didn't seem much to talk about. It seemed so unconnected to anything in any of our lives.

A month afterward, in February, Larry Schneider moved out of the house. Lina said he was living in his garage, which was the only thing in the world that meant anything to him anyway. That was the only thing she said.

Our block, predominantly Catholic, had never before seen a marriage break up. Larry had always been considered so strange that no one thought to look for a reason for what he did. Or maybe they did, and just didn't talk to my mother about it. Of all the women on the block, only Lina and my mother weren't part of the kaffeeklatsch.

When was it, what time of the year, how much time passed between Larry's leaving the house and Lina coming to ask my mother the favor? It wasn't a favor for herself; she said it was for Jack, her old friend Jack who'd shouted her name from the car on New Year's Eve. Jack was leaving his wife. Yes, there were children; all the money would go to them. The wife was a monster, a tormenter. His heart was broken to be leaving his children, but on the other hand, she'd turned them against him anyway. He was in a terrible position. Lina felt she had to give him a hand. And would we give him a hand too? If we'd rent him the spare bedroom, and allow him bathroom privileges, he could take his meals with her next door.

Not for a second did my mother share with me a suspicion that Jack Henderson's leaving his wife had something to do with Larry Schneider's moving into his garage. My mother agreed to the arrangement with Jack, even though it meant Jack and I would have to share a bathroom. When I brought this up, my mother said she hadn't thought of it. I had a point, she said. I'd have to use the downstairs bathroom which was smaller. It didn't have a tub, only a stall shower, which I didn't like nearly so well. I was afraid to object, afraid we'd lose money we needed because of my objections. And I didn't want to displease Lina; neither of us did. Her suggestions felt like orders, although the source of her authority was never clear. It was just that military bearing. That naval stance.

I've never seen a man as clean-looking as Jack Henderson. He had an immaculate, knifelike profile, a raised mole above his upper lip that seemed polished, or buffed. His hair was clipped short; his shoes were shined like mirrors. He wore a leather fedora which he kept on as he walked up the stairs to his room.

The floor of his room was covered with gray linoleum. He didn't even put a mat beside his bed. He didn't have a bedspread, just a navy blue blanket with a darker navy blue stripe halfway across its expanse. No satin bindings, nothing ornamental, softened the blanket. He left nothing in the bathroom, no toothbrush, toothpaste, soap, razor, or comb. He left his towel folded on the radiator beside his bed. I knew all this because he'd ask me to leave any mail that came for him on his dresser. Occasionally, there were letters from his lawyers. I assumed they were re: the Henderson divorce.

After another while, perhaps it was six months, Jack no longer came back to his room, the room in our house, to

sleep. Once, with the coarse knowingness of a young virgin, I said to my mother, "Well, I guess we know what
he's doing at night," and my mother slapped me. "She
makes a big meal for him, he works hard all day, he gets
drowsy, he falls asleep on the couch. If he wakes up in the
middle of the night he doesn't want to come all the way
over here; he's considerate, he doesn't want to wake us, so
he just goes up to Lina's boys' old room."

Both the boys were gone. Robbie was in the navy in
Vietnam. Tommy, the older one, had tried to go into the
marines, but was rejected because of his poor eyesight. He
was living in the garage with his father. They were
reported to be living in incredible filth; their hair grew
down to their shoulders, they let their beards grow. They
looked wild, like mountain men. Someone said they
brought prostitutes in to stay with them; someone else
said the old father, paralyzed, was down there with them.
But no one knew. Rich men with their rare expensive
cars still brought their engines to him; it was said he was a
genius.

Cindi was still a child and so she was at home, but as
her mother said, she never thought of anything but
horses. She competed on light, quick mounts, but she
herself was a workhorse. She always seemed to be pulling
something heavy behind her—a wagon full of hay, and
her eyes had the sweet dull sorrowful look of animals
who work too hard.

"I simply refuse to believe that she'd be doing anything with a man in the same house with her daughter,"
my mother said, putting an end to the discussion. She

continued to take Jack's rent money, although he never used the room. Occasionally, he went up there and stayed a little while.

But only I knew why.

It is not unknown, the sexual curiosity of well-behaved young girls that leads them to breach the commonest, the most basic laws of civilization. That makes them look where they know they are forbidden, where anyone would be forbidden. The right running of the world is based on the belief that it keeps itself in good order precisely so that such young girls will not know about the things that they already know, that they'll do anything to see the proof of. The cold, feverish eyes of law-abiding girls. The eyes that often make them sorry.

What made me think it was permissible for me to go through Jack Henderson's drawers one day when I left an envelope on his dresser? Did I hesitate? Did I turn back, leave the room, go into my own room or down the stairs, into the kitchen or the downstairs bathroom, which I continued to use to the exclusion of the upstairs one, although it had been years since Jack had used it? I only know that one day (it was cold, the sounds of my heels rang off the gray linoleum like horse's hooves on freezing stone), I opened his drawers. Found handkerchiefs, perfectly folded. A few shirts. Two sweaters, in a drawer of their own. And then, in the bottom, a collection of books I knew were there because they needed to be hidden.

Of course I opened them, and read. Or glanced, because I knew what I was looking for would be found quickly. Only, I imagined that what I was looking for would be somehow recognizable to me. But what I found crushed my imagination. It wasn't the feather touch of titillation, or the quick chase of arousal, but the paralyzing force of a puzzlement so deep that the mind feels like a locked machine, seized up, incapable of motion. All those books—there were at least ten of them—had the same subject. A group of lesbians kidnap a young boy, dress him as a girl, beat him, and then have sex with him. Ten books, all with the same narrative. Where did Jack Henderson find them? How did he know where to look?

I couldn't understand that these books were about sex, which I had assumed to be connected to men staring at the breasts and crotches of naked women, and then pene-trating them. It was about something much stronger than sex, something that excluded me, something that made me curse my looking, and know that I would never look in the same way again. But I would never, I promised, never look at Jack Henderson's things ever again. I vowed that.

But, of course, I did look again, I looked several times. The last time I opened the drawer, all the books were gone. We had a secret, Jack and I, a real secret, genuinely untellable. I thought that one day he'd exact a price from me, which I would have no choice but to pay. But that never happened. In all the years I knew him, Jack Henderson and I exchanged only the most commonplace of greetings or remarks.

*   *   *

The sixties hammered on. I went to college. Lina allowed her beautiful long legs to be revealed by shorter and shorter skirts; she wore her hair in higher and higher and more stiffly lacquered constructions. Cindi wore nothing but loose blue jeans and plaid men's shirts. Her hair hung down her back, despondent, downhearted, like the hair of those who fear their mother doesn't want the sight of them before her brilliant eyes.

Lina studied to become a practical nurse; Larry continued to make a fortune, but gave her no money. I guess he knew that with Jack living with her, Lina didn't have much legal recourse.

It was lucky for me, Lina's decision to get nurse's training, because in those years with my mother drinking so heavily, I often needed her help when my mother fell. I would leave my mother on the floor, and go next door where I would knock for Lina. She never made me say anything. We did what needed to be done.

Those years, when she saw me, Lina focused on my clothes. If she saw me with a new outfit, she always praised me. And I knew what her praise meant. She knew I had, like her, a life that had something to do with pleasing men, not only with serving them. That had to do with being pleased by them as well. Looking around at the neighbor women, standing heavily in their doors in the morning, holding their half-filled coffee cups, Lina and I knew we shared something. She didn't know what I shared with her man.

We both knew Cindi didn't share it. Right after high school, Cindi became the first mounted policewoman in Queens. She was absolutely happy in her work. Each morning, she drove off in her uniform, her hip boots shining, her holster strapped to her uninflected waist.

I moved away, lived in different cities, got married, and quickly divorced. When I came home after the divorce— the first in our family—Lina told my mother to look all the neighbors and the relatives in the face and spit in their eyes. My mother kept saying, "I can't understand it. I just can't understand it." But Lina understood. I didn't have to tell her I had left my husband for another man.

Cindi began dating an insurance man twenty years older than her, who wore patent leather ankle boots and white socks that peeked above them. His hands were small and very white. As they would leave the house to go out on their dates, Cindi would say with a false jokiness that filled me with foreboding, "Let's go, guy."

Lina had an engagement party for Cindi. I think it was the first party in the house since the New Year's Eve when Jack Henderson had cried her name over and over into the January air. I was invited to see Cindi try on her wedding dress, a dispiriting sight. She was a girl who lacked exactly that fantastic element that a bride's gown requires. Lina and Cindi, who'd grown close over the elaborate wedding preparations, were delighted with the dress.

But the wedding didn't come off. Two days before, the groom sent a note, saying he just couldn't, he was going

back to Texas, to his family. Lina had to return all the pres-
ents to the people who'd brought them to the house on
the night of Cindi's party.

She told my mother it was the hardest thing she'd ever
done.

THE
ARCHITECTURE
OF A
LIFE WITH PRIESTS

My parents were introduced by a priest; their first meeting took place in a convent. My mother was visiting Father B., who was preaching for the nuns. And my father had written him a letter of violent criticism, attacking Father B. for his too left-wing tolerance for other faiths, accusing him of being careless of the treasure my father had newly been allowed access to as a result of his conversion. No longer a Jew, and only recently allowed to use the coin of the realm, he wished to insure its value. Intrigued by my father's vituperative eloquence, Father B. arranged to meet him at the Convent of Mary Reparatrix on Twenty-ninth Street. My mother, I believe, never thought of criticizing a priest, nor writing a letter to an author. Priests embodied her idea of the desirable male, but without the danger to her integrity of desire. They were observable only from a distance, like movie stars; they were garbed like kings or like Jesus himself; they listened to her sorrows and forgave her sins without revealing any of their sorrows or suggesting their capacity for sinfulness. She passed it on to me, this habit of worshiping a princely caste, the sickish feeling of delight when you were singled out by a priest, the shutting down of the iron door on bleeding fingers when you were unnoticed, or (unthinkable) castigated.

It is odd, and oddly appropriate, that my parents met in a convent rather than a monastery: a dwelling run by women who were consecrated to live lives without a man. My mother had no romance about nuns, no friends among nuns. What could they give her that she couldn't get in a better place? She had a mother, she had sisters: what she needed was a man to worship. In her austere, imperial mother she had all the material for adoration she would need; in her sisters, the uneasy peerage, the shared fellowship in tasks that a community of women in vows might provide. But her father, short, sickly, and ill-tempered, didn't emit the stuff she needed for her dreams. For this, she required priests.

And yet, how much I owe to that convent! Not only my existence, in providing a place for my parents to meet, but an image that has allowed me an ideal by which I have always measured myself. In the chapel of the Convent of Mary Reparatrix, when I was three years old, I saw a young nun kneeling in a pool of light. The habits of the Sisters of Mary Reparatrix, a French order (does this account for their fashionableness?), were an extraordinary color for nuns. They were a royal blue, no, a cross between royal and sky, not aqua, not turquoise—they suggested nothing of the sea—but they were darker than any element that clouds could be a part of. Kneeling in light, the light falling on the pure blue of her habit, the whiteness of her hands, bouncing off her glasses, this nun knelt and showed me all I needed to know of perfect form. Her spine was perfectly straight; her shoes were invisible beneath her long skirts; her hands, white, were symmetrically folded (my first lesson in the Gothic). On one finger she wore the gold ring of her marriage to Christ. She was entirely still, and we were nothing to her; she was her function: a pray-er, one who prayed. She was a vessel emptied of herself, at once the model for the artist and the work of art. When I have tried to give myself over—to love, or work, to the task of attentiveness, to the discipline of looking or of waiting, to the humility of rendering without the consciousness of how what I render will be received—I think of that nun, nameless, faceless, kneeling in her pool of light.

But Mary Reparatrix is the only convent where anything important happened to us. We did not visit convents, because we were not a family with interest in nuns. My romance of nuns came only from the movies: Audrey Hepburn, Ingrid Bergman. The nuns who taught me every day no more suggested the romance of the religious life than my mother suggested the romance of heterosexual coupling. They were too near, they were too busy, they were not beautiful, they were ill-educated, they were lower class. More mercifully put: they were overworked to the point of exploitation. In my classrooms, there were never less than fifty children; children shared seats and textbooks, and the nuns, often too young or too old for the job, had had no training. I wasn't lucky in the order of nuns who taught me; had I had the elegant Ursulines or

Madames of the Sacred Heart, thin-fingered daughters of privilege giving up a comfortable life for the cool polish of the cloister, I might have wished to see myself in them. But the nuns who taught me were workhorses, or work mares, and above all I had no interest in that. Besides, nuns didn't like me, because although I was obedient, intelligent, devout, I was incurably untidy and only one of them (but this was later, when I was a teenager) was able to get past that to see that I might be of any value.

We didn't visit convents, but we did visit monasteries. This is because of my mother's connection to the priests of a particular order, half-cloistered, half in the world, the Passionist Fathers, who were devoted to the Suffering and Death of Christ. And my mother was devoted to them.

They wore long black robes cinched with a wide leather belt, and over their breasts a stylized black-and-white leather heart, with the initials JXP, which stood for something about Jesus' Passion. They wore sandals, and in the monastery their feet were always bare. Their motto was "We Preach Christ Crucified." That is, their mission was to preach; eloquence was their vocation, not the terror-inducing eloquence of the Redemptionists; not the continental suaveness of the Jesuits, but the plain, restated call: Christ Suffered and Died for You.

Was my mother devoted to the order because she was devoted to particular men there? Or did she like their message and its medium? Or was it that she liked the idea of a group of monks—the Passionists happened to be only semicloistered, and their motherhouse was within seven miles of our home. Whatever the reason, iconic,

geographical, she and my father felt it was a worthwhile
and ennobling trip to drive the miles to the Monastery of
the Immaculate Conception.

We always went at night; I have no memory of seeing
the church in daylight. And I have no memory of going
to the large upstairs church; we always attended devotions
or stations of the cross downstairs, in the church reserved
for the priests and their guests. I don't think we ever went
to Mass there. We would make the Stations, or have Benediction, or the Novena to Our Lady of the Miraculous
Medal. It was exciting to be in a church when it was a
part of the darkness. When the panes of the stained-glass
window didn't glow like jewels but stored light inside
them like flat rhomboids of lead. In the darkness, it
seemed that the incense and smoke from the snuffed can-
dles penetrated our clothing and our skin with a direct-
ness and a thoroughness they could not have in the light
of day.

We would be shown into the vestibule of the
monastery by a lay brother, and there, on hard leather
benches, I would watch the dim light from the ceiling
fixture fall on the polished floor, making dull pools of
illumination that seemed, in their muteness, to be telling
me a greater truth about the shedding of light that I,
ignorant, could not grasp. Behind the closed door, I
would hear the *flap-flap* of the monks' sandals on the
floor's hard surface; I would hear the swinging of their
beads. Their voices, low and male, the voices that could by
their power turn bread and wine into the body and blood
of Christ, seeped through the door in a deep buzz. Then

the door would open, Father L. would come through, open his arms to embrace us, and show us to his office.

Father L. seemed to be more cheerful than the other Passionists, more playful and more informal, as if he'd mistakenly got himself into the wrong order; he didn't have the face for preaching Christ crucified, he liked jokes, and he had a stash of cookies he could hardly wait to offer me. He'd been to Rome to study, was an expert in canon law, but for some reason it has only now occurred to me to consider strange (perhaps it was his cheerfulness, his personableness, that qualified him), his job was to run the branch of the order devoted to Mass cards and a "perpetual prayer society." The objective correlative of this society was a leatherette booklet with a choice of pictures (The Agony In the Garden, the Sacred Heart, the Assumption) and the name of the deceased inscribed in illuminated script, on top of the assurance that the named would have a share in the prayers of the Passionist order for all eternity. These booklets were called, for some reason only obliquely clear to me, purgatorials. They could be bought for five dollars.

I now remember why we visited Father L. so often. The reason was this: my mother, in order to help the order, would take boxes of purgatorials and sell them to friends and business contacts who wanted to bring to a funeral an offering more impressive than an ordinary Mass card. So I never thought it odd when someone, a stranger, would come to the door, and say, "I'm here for a purgatorial." I would get my mother, she would reach into the cardboard box, and with a special pen, inscribe the deceased's name in the blank space above the illuminated text. She would take the five dollars, and mail it to Father L.

Father L.'s office was unlovely and functional; there were metal cabinets and metal tables and fluorescent lights buzzed above gray linoleum. He offered me coconut cookies which I disliked, and brown-edged wafers which I adored. Despite the inequality of my response, I feared rudeness morbidly, and always took one of each, hating myself and the coconut cookies for their disgusting texture, which reminded me of cuticles of bitten nails. I would be asked to sing a song for Father L. and he would clap and smile. My father's role was gently to criticize Father L. for his choice in religious art: why, my father asked, not try to elevate the taste of the faithful. Father L. agreed but said they were running a business. He tactfully never mentioned my father's business in religious cards and stationery that had, crashingly, failed.

I was happy in that room, in the dark lit by fluorescence, with the grayness punctuated only by crucifixes, with Father L.'s bare white feet in his hard black sandals, and the coarse fabric of his habit, and the cookies he put in an envelope that said *Passionist Fathers* for me to take home. Occasionally, he would show my father one of his old books, in Latin, of canon law. Once he told us he prayed every day for the soul of Harry Houdini.

Why is it that I have much clearer memories of Immaculate Conception church and of Father L.'s office than I have of our parish church? I know it was torn down some time before my father's death, that is, before I was seven, but I have memories only of some objects that adorned it—ironwork, holy water fonts, bowls screwed to the wall with a cross their only ornament—and the poor box, with its slot and iron lettering FOR THE POOR. I remember the shape of the pews, but not the colors of any of the stained-glass windows. For a few years, we had Mass in the school auditorium, and of that I remember only a large stage where the altar was placed, light wooden floors, and windows barred to keep away destructive basketballs, because when the auditorium wasn't being a church, it was a gym. I don't remember which place—the old church or the auditorium—held my First Communion.

There should be a catalogue of forgetting, simply a list of names which carry with them no images. Followed by speculations upon why the name has lodged in the brain, an empty vessel, a gourd rattling around a few dry seeds. The church was one; my First Communion was another. I remember not the day, only the preparations.

Because it was an entirely sacred day, everything connected to it seemed sacred. The morning of my First Communion our apartment seemed to have become sanctified. The light came in—bluish, tinged with sacramental content, traveling straight from the underwing of the Holy Spirit. I woke terrified. Suppose I accidentally put some food in my mouth? Suppose I accidentally popped a grape or chomped on a roll or a piece of celery? It would be all over. I would not be allowed to process with my class. I could take Communion on some other day, but privately, and without honor. Oh, we were honored, we were pure, we had been purified, we would never be so pure again. I was in love with my own hunger, with the dryness of my mouth, which I would not relieve with water, although water was allowed.

Holiest of all were the things specially procured for my First Communion. My white organdy gloves. My blue-and-white-lacquered prayer book with the picture of the Virgin spreading her voluminous skirts, the white ribbon to mark my place, the gold edge of the pages. The veil, which I dreamed of and which was not a disappointment when it came, although the plastic headband dug into my skull; nevertheless, when I walked, behind me floated the stiff but airy gauziness properly belonging to a bride. My dress, though, was a disappointment, because it was created not to please me, but to prove my mother's and grandmother's rectitude, their revolt against a purely female exhibition, their stand taken against vanity and display, their taste for the austere rather than the "show-off." I'd dreamed of a dress with wide, stiff skirts, layers of lace, and flounces. "You want to look like one of those Italians?" my mother asked. And immediately I saw a world divided in two, the dark world of the Italians, the lower world, the world drained of spirit, where what was left was heavy as the flesh, slow moving, and susceptible to corruption, a climatic zone where disease could easily breed, the lush growth only a sign of danger, not to be reveled in but shunned. The other world had the clarity of an Irish morning; its lines were true, and unobscured; the

light fell straight upon it, no deceiving shadows lurked, no
surface where living horrors might breed, eat in, destroy.
When I looked at my face, my dark hair, my dark eyes, my
large features, I saw nothing that reminded me of Ireland.
But I didn't want the fleshy world of heavy sauces and
superstitions, of women who said the Rosary out loud
during Mass instead of following the Latin in their prayer
books. I looked like my father, but how could I think of
myself in terms of my Jewish-born father when I was
planning my First Communion dress? So I gave in to my
mother's and grandmother's wishes, hopelessly, soaked in
disappointment, feeling I was meant to represent something I couldn't possibly represent, feeling unclothed and
vulnerable in my dress with its drop waist and thin sash,
envying, even as I was contemptuous of, the full and
cumbrous skirts of my peers, standing for something I
knew to be inferior but desired, impossibly, with all my
heart.

Vague about my old parish church, I have clearer memories of a church in the next town, a church my aunt and
uncle and their children went to, where my mother would
take me to daily Mass. It was a stone church, small and
dark. Our Lady of Lourdes it was called, and it had something of the feeling of a grotto. I was always sleepy at that
Mass; I'd been yanked out of bed, dressed quickly, my hair
roughly brushed (my mother was in a hurry, she could just
"squeeze Mass in" on her way to work), and the gray light
that seemed to me to be coming from the stones rather

than the windows reminded me of my sleep life, dun colored, entirely desirable, of which I longed to be again a part. I was too young for Communion, so I sat and watched the people. They all seemed very old. One woman, who wore the low-heeled black oxfords all old ladies wore in those days, and a black felt hat with an amber-colored feather and an ornamental hat pin, had a growth on her nose, hard and purple and the size of a plum. I admired her courage in appearing in the world with it, but I hated her for forcing me to see her affliction. I prayed for her; I prayed for myself, to be forgiven my unworthy thoughts, but I was frightened that in the time I was alone in the pew, the time it took my mother to come back from the Communion rail, she'd approach me and, somehow, touch me with her disfigurement, forcing me to be disfigured as she was.

There was a way in which the sacred spaces that we lived by were transportable, or portable, and that is because every place a priest visited, every place he stopped or stayed, became, by that virtue, and for those hours, sacred. A priest was consecrate, he was anointed, this was not an abstraction but an act that had happened in time and space. At the time of his ordination, a young man, a healthy animal (why do I think always of a calf being led through a Swiss meadow garlanded, his horns painted gold), had his hands bound with strips of white linen cloth and his temples anointed with holy oil. The mark was considered—the word had the thrill of doom on it—

indelible. Thou art a priest forever. Oh the number of dramas and melodramas about the indelible mark of priesthood—legible through drunkenness, and fornication, and betrayal of the name of the Lord—to the moment of death and then to all eternity!

So when they visited us, the priests brought their sacredness into our home with them. Many of them seemed uncomfortable in a domestic situation, but of all the priests who visited us, Father B. was most dramatically homeless, most clearly expressed the disconnected state of priests, their rootlessness, their life of service rather than domestic habitation. He was a Passionist, but I don't know where he was stationed, what his motherhouse was. How the two dictions come together—"stationed": the military; "motherhouse": the child, protected by an endlessly nurturing, endlessly replenishing home.

Father B. had introduced my parents and had baptized me. But my father didn't like him. He said it was because he was a "liberal," but I wonder if it was more, I wonder if it was Father B.'s androgynous but sexy lower lip, like a girlish Richard Burton's, whether it was the fact that, with Father B. in the room, I was drawn to a male body other than my father's.

Father B. was the only man I'd ever met who conformed to my idea of handsomeness, whose looks seemed something like a movie star's. And so I was excited in his presence; I was a fan, and my father, who knew me very well, must have sensed my excitement and despised it, since he would have understood its source. When he ate dinner at our house, Father B. would lean back in his chair to tell a joke. He loved jokes, he collected them for his sermons and the Communion breakfasts at which he was always being paid to speak. My father didn't approve of jokes in sermons. Father B. would stick his arm out into the room and impatiently wiggle his fingers, as if he were making room for someone to snuggle in beside him. I always wanted to be sitting on his lap, and my father disliked this. "Don't maul the man," he said to me once, in a rare burst of disapproval. I yearned for Father B.'s visits and cried when he left but I have no memory of what happened when I was actually with him.

But I remember my father taking Father B. into his room to argue, closing the door, and shouting words like *orthodox,* and *heresy,* which I would hear from where I sat on the threshold of the room. I folded my hands in prayer and squeezed them together, as if the small pain would be a further proof of the seriousness of my intention. I was praying that we wouldn't have to pay for my father's bad behavior to a priest.

After they were through with their arguing, my father and Father B. would come out into the hall. And what happened then would alarm me more than anything. My father would fall to his knees and ask Father B. for his blessing. Father B. would place his hands on my father's head, whisper some Latin words, and make the sign of the cross above him.

I knew everything this was supposed to mean: that it didn't matter that my father had insulted Father B. *as a man;* the office of the priesthood was infinitely respectable and humbling to him. My father had no hesitation about falling to his knees. But I hated it. I didn't believe in the possibility of this division of identity—the object of scorn, the sacred vessel; the persecutor, the humble penitent—although it was part of my faith to do so. I didn't like seeing my father on his knees, and I didn't like Father B.'s hands raised above him. In resisting this tableau I knew that I transgressed, but I felt I was right, and my sense of my rightness was the first window letting in a disturbing light that fell straight onto the white stone of ancient practice.

Father B. was known for his charity, particularly to old widows, and my mother would often drive him to take tea with one of them. All of the houses were one house; with old-fashioned Persian carpets, gentle watercolors with pictures of cows drinking from brooks, a print of the Good Shepherd, which always struck me as vaguely Protestant because that image of Jesus was too unphysical, with no sense of agony or violence—qualities I connected with the Christ who was worshiped in my house. We would drink tea from thin cups; the cookies, which they would take from round tins, always seemed a little stale, as if they'd been saved for months just for this occasion, as if the widows or the spinsters had deprived themselves to save the treat for Father. I relieved my boredom by staring at Father B., occasionally sitting on his lap, although I saw my hostesses didn't like that. Father B. never seemed to notice, and I pretended not to.

He had an old mother who lived in a huge, windowless apartment in Hoboken. My mother would drive him there, through the Lincoln Tunnel, past the rock wall next to a sign pointing to Weehawken, a name that filled me with alarm, as though there were still Indians there waiting to scalp us if we made the wrong turn. From that road, we could see the glittering skyline of Manhattan, distant as a lunar landscape. We were going in the opposite direction, to New Jersey, to the house of an old woman. No Broadway shows for us, no hamburgers in restaurants, no ice cream served by Irish waitresses in Schraft's. We were doing works of charity.

The walls of Father B.'s mother's apartment were stucco, a dark rose, and this seemed inappropriate, too worldly, too sexy for the mother of a priest. She dressed in the long-waisted fashions of the twenties, and her hair was set in deep archaic waves. She wore too much lipstick and rouge, and her features were overlarge, like the Red Queen's in *Alice in Wonderland*. There were photographs of Father B., a three year old in long curls, high-buttoned shoes, and a large, ornate bow tie. There was a photo of a dog, and I was afraid to ask if it was one that had belonged to them.

Father B.'s mother's name was Jennie and my mother said she might be English. Altogether, I found her the wrong mother for her elegant son, who wrote me letters and once sent me a chocolate valentine in the mail.

After small talk, Father B. would clear space on the dresser and say Mass. I would kneel on the floor; my mother couldn't kneel and his mother was too old. Before my First Communion, I looked up hungrily at my fortunate elders, longing, like a princess, for my coronation. After First Communion, I was allowed to hold the plate

under the others' chins. Father B. would disappear into
the dark kitchen and wash the sacred vessels—paten,
chalice, pyx—he had taken from his black bag, the bag
that looked like a doctor's, then repack them in their
leather pouch and replace them, covering them with a
book in case thieves should break in. After the ritual
moment, the apartment became its ordinary cavernous
self; the light of the sacrament went out, and it was only a
place inhabited by an old lady, with the unfresh smell of
overworn taffeta and perfume with a used floral scent.

   When I was in my twenties and Father B., in his sixties, was dying of cancer, he actually spent the night in my
mother's and my house. Was it that, so near death, he was
considered by his superiors safe to be alone in a house
with women? Before he went to bed he asked my mother
to massage his shoulders. He wouldn't ask, he said, only
he could barely stand the pain. I slept with my mother in
her bed that night, and above us he coughed and paced
the floor and we could hear him use the toilet. Neither of
us below could sleep. In the morning, we served him
breakfast at the kitchen table, knowing that he would
never break bread—the Sacred Bread of the Host, the
ordinary bread of ordinary mealtimes—with us, or for us,
again.

ooooooooooooooo

Father D. inhabited my life long before I met him, like a
character of myth or legend, from one of the lives of the
saints or an adventure film. He was my mother's confessor, the preacher whom the working women followed in

order that they would be able to make his retreats. My mother had been active in what was known as the working women's retreat movement. I am always amused and surprised by the unfamiliarity to most people of certain words that I use automatically. Retreat, for example. I have to understand that I am writing the history of another country, and above all, a country with another language, and that the concept of a retreat is as foreign to most people as a glove compartment or a trunk might be to a future generation that has passed right through the age of the automobile, and knows only of space travel. All the words that shaped us—"Sacramental," "Occasion of Sin," "Fast Days," "Feast Days," "State of Grace"—were not unusual or difficult or complex in themselves but they opened a world. Or a door, a door straight to a past which had in actuality been over hundreds of years, but seemed, when we went through the door, a road we could walk down, a meadow we could easily luxuriate in, a truer, richer home. When most of my friends hear *retreat,* they think of a cabin in the pines surrounded by air and silence. For Catholics, a retreat is a time of concentrated prayer, away from others, to be sure, but spiritually labor intensive, a decathlon for the soul. Groups of the devout, sometimes the penitent, gather to hear sermons, to read holy books, to pray, and to confess.

In the thirties, working women were seen to be particularly in need of such a getaway, or such renewal. My mother's life outside her family—and that she had a life outside the family was made possible by its spiritual center—was built around these retreats. She would drive,

sometimes taking her mother, sometimes not, many hundreds of miles to convents where retreats were given. My
mother drove through all kinds of weather to meet with
other women from the Northeast under the direction of
one priest whom they followed with a devotion only just
short of idolatry. Wherever Father D. was giving a retreat,
a knot of women from New York, New Jersey, Connecti-
cut, and Massachusetts followed.

It is not clear to me, in the triangle of my mother and
my father and Father D., who was the most loving and
who the most beloved and in which direction the arrows
of love flew. My mother introduced him to my father and
from that time on her relationship to him was eclipsed by
his adoration of her boyfriend, who became her husband,
then the father of her child. When my parents asked his
advice about marrying he told them not to. He said that
my father's mind and his work must not be held back by
the worldly concerns of a husband. When I was a
teenager, I found the letter he wrote my mother on the
occasion of my father's death: "Say nothing to me of your
grief," he wrote, "you, at least, had a child of his loins. I
have nothing."

The first place I felt the sacralizing power of his spirit
was a phone booth in a drugstore. My mother's two best
friends, her friends from the working women's retreats,
would come out to our house from Brooklyn and the
Bronx, ostensibly to have dinner with my mother and
me, but really to "place a long distance call," to Father D.
They never did it in the house with my grandmother and
my aunt; they always went to the drugstore in the build-

ing where my mother's office was. One at a time, they would get into the wooden booth, surrounded by displays presenting bottles of mouthwash, cans of hair spray. They'd close the doors that folded in the center like a stiff accordion, and have their private conversations with him. Did they choose this situation because it most closely replicated the confessional? I, too, was allowed my moment in the "booth," in which I spoke to a stranger, whose dark, hawklike face I knew from photographs. I said I was fine, that I did well in school, that I was saying my prayers.

The distance the telephone signal traveled must have given the situation an added glamour, for Father D. lived in places none of these women had ever been, exotic places—Albuquerque, New Mexico, Sudbury, Ontario. The year that I was born, Father D. had fought with his superiors about the increasing liberalism of the Passionist order. He walked out of the monastery one night, and from a pay phone in Springfield, Massachusetts, called the Bishop of Albuquerque, volunteering to work among the Indians. He never went back to the monastery. He sent us beaded necklaces and headbands from New Mexico; he wrote, describing his plans to set up cooperative groceries, to have the people build their own church (he was an expert carpenter and mechanic) including a form of air-conditioning that worked without electricity, using only the moisture in the air. I don't know why he left Albuquerque—it was under some cloud—but the next thing we knew he was in Sudbury, Ontario, until, one summer, he phoned to say he was coming for a visit.

My mother phoned me at the camp run by her family. She was coming up, and she was bringing her two friends from the working women's retreat. Father D. would join them.

Instantly, my status at the camp changed. I was moved from my grandmother's room in the house where all the campers were cooked for, and ate, to the guest house at the top of the hill. The afternoon he was meant to arrive, I was sent down to the property gate on the highway. I was to direct him up the hill to the place where the women were waiting for him as the Jacobites waited for Bonnie Prince Charlie.

He drove up in the first foreign car I had ever seen driven by someone I knew. It was as though he'd driven straight from Europe, over the ocean to the place where I stood. He stopped as soon as he saw me, he leaned over and opened the door. For a moment, neither of us said anything. We looked at each other in silence. Then he spoke. "So you are Mary Catherine," he said.

No one ever called me by my full baptismal name. I knew he was doing it because I was my father's daughter, and it seemed thrillingly correct. I nodded, yes, I was. He made a sweeping gesture in the direction of the passenger's seat. I got into the car. Silently we drove up the hill, the women were standing in the doorway. They had been cooking all day.

We provided our own food, but my aunt brought, every morning, bottles of cold milk. I was allowed to have the cream off the top of the milk for my cereal—Frosted Flakes which were permitted me on the intercession of my mother's friends, who said this was a special time, and I was to be given a treat.

But before breakfast, a white linen cloth was laid on the rough pine table, the chairs were moved away, my aunts and my uncles and my mother's friends knelt on the pine boards to pray and receive the sacrament. The transformation seemed to me enormous; the house was so rural, so having to do with nature, so American, with its fieldstones and its pine beams and the moose head and the Adirondack bentwood furniture. Suddenly, history, and Europe and salvation, entered the wood smoke–saturated air; wine was consumed and so was the unnourishing Host. Outside, I heard the boy campers shouting and laughing on their way to the activities I dreaded: arts and crafts, ball playing, nature lore. I covered my face with my hands, relishing my deliverance, my presence in a shelter, away from trees and rocks and most especially those boys. When Father D. gave me Communion, he lay his hand on top of my head and left it there an extra second. He did this to no one else.

From the moment he met me, he anointed me with his anointing. His eyes would fill with tears if suddenly I had a look that brought to mind my deceased father. He was so thoroughly masculine, so Greek or Indian in his stoicism, that his tears had a particular value, like the tears wrung from the agonized Christ in the Garden.

After he left the camp, he drove to Miami, where he stayed for some months, then to assist an old friend of his, another ex-Passionist, in a rectory in Paterson, New Jersey. My mother, her two friends, and I drove there one

Friday night a month. We took him to an Italian restau-
rant; we sat in his office in the rectory, bare except for fil-
ing cabinets and a steel safe, with a picture of the
Crucifixion and one of the Madonna, where the phone
would ring with news that someone had died or requests
for information on the time of Masses. We would travel
from the office in Father D.'s sacerdotal wake, into the
church where he would perform benediction and we
would sing "O Salutaris," and "Tantum Ergo," recite the
Litany of the Divine Praises, bow our heads before the
censed Host in the monstrance like a starburst, and then
return to the rectory, for whiskey and snacks—but I was
given Cokes, which Father D. procured for me only.

After a year, he fought with his old friend, and moved up
to his brother's home in Elmira, New York. His brother,
whom he'd seen only a handful of times in the thirty
years since his ordination, contacted him after he had a
heart attack. The visit produced a new living situation:
Father D. would live in his brother's house, would help,
using the money he earned "freelancing" from local
parishes, with its upkeep, and would do the work that the
large house required for its good maintenance.

There's a mystery that can surround or locate itself at
the center of a house's life. It was there in my grandmother's house, and I recognize it when I think of Father
D. and his brother. The house's very structure, the number
or arrangement of its rooms, has a powerful effect upon

the decisions people make by which they live and know themselves. Had Father D.'s brother not had a large house, large enough twenty years earlier, to have comfortably housed three daughters—all with their own rooms—and in addition had a basement, an attic, a garage, all of which needed attending when they fell into ordinary disrepair— Father D.'s decision to live with his brother after an estrangement of thirty years would not have been made. The force of stone, and brick, and beams, and flooring seem to crush the possibility of questions: why are you living as you do, or to provide an answer, beyond which anything else seems finicking and overly complex: "Because there is room to."

Father D.'s brother's house was the first house I thought of as being completely American, perhaps because it was the first house I spent time in that was any distance from New York. The trees seemed connected to the American dream of endless forest tamed for the domestic comfort of the newly prosperous. You couldn't imagine anyone on those streets speaking in a foreign accent. You couldn't imagine the smell of garlic or of spices that would cover or disguise the good meat that had only recently grazed so near, the clean milk, the abundant golden butter, the white bread, soft and virtu- ally crustless, the desserts of Jell-O or ice cream or a large voluptuous layer cake inhabiting a glass-domed dish. No one would shout on these streets, in these houses, although they might beat each other to death and hide the bodies in the basements. There was no way of telling

who was Catholic and who Protestant. The lawns in front
of each house were identical as were the rounded, modest, unassertive shrubs.

In Father D.'s brother's house there were things I'd
only read about in magazines—a BarcaLounger, a breakfast nook. On either side of the benches that made up the
breakfast nook—an impractical arrangement because
whoever seated himself first was trapped—there was a
photograph, entirely covering the wall, of a scene of
autumn foliage. There were no radiators, therefore no
need for me to worry whether the correct pronunciation
was with a long or a short *a*, a distinction I knew meant
something, although I did not know what. Instead there
were only ornamental iron gratings, called, remarkably to
me, registers; grating-covered holes in the floor through
which hot air, heated by the furnace in the basement, rose
up within a jacket surrounding the furnace, traveling
through pipes that led up to the registers. You could close
the register with a lever you moved with your toe, forbidding heat, or open it, inviting heat into the place you
were.

We didn't stay in the house. But Father D.'s sister-in-
law was grateful to the point of stupefaction and adored
him, as every woman (including myself) who came near
him did? And so she felt she had to provide food for us.
We stayed at a motel and arrived at the house for breakfast. Father D.'s sister-in-law had already gone to work;
she was a foreman in a box factory, the only regular wage
earner in the house. When she came home, Father D.
would engage with her in domestic teasing, accusing her

of being too fussy about details of housekeeping, insisting that he could do all her work in a third the time, and make everyone happier. Sometimes she would let him cook, but she didn't like his spicy concoctions, although we preferred them, but, good guests, would not say so.

The summer I was twelve I was invited to stay there a month. I don't know what anyone could have been thinking. My days were filled with boredom; I walked around the neighborhood. Lost in America. I walked to the local swimming pool, where I disconsolately swam laps and failed the challenge I set for myself to dive off the high diving board. In the morning I made my bed, went to Mass with Father D., watched while he did his chores, and read my books. In the afternoon I walked, engulfed in loneliness, or swam. In the evenings, I helped Father D. make supper and listened as he talked. He gave me books of theology to read—Karl Adam on the Eucharist—which were too hard for me, although I didn't admit it. He would ask me if I liked the book, and I'd say yes, though he never asked me if I understood it or what it was I liked. After supper, I would lie in my own bed, guiltily reading books about nurses and the doctors that they loved, and in the morning I would start the day with prayer and live it out in silence. When my mother came, I felt liberated by the declericalization of my world; I knew I'd failed the test of the austere, serious life Father D. had set for me, although I was proud I had kept my failure from him.

After a few years, when the sister-in-law saw that our visits were becoming a pattern, we never went to the house; we stayed at the motel all day, except for Mass and to go out for food. In the anonymous rooms made for illicit coupling or cheap family vacations, we sat—the women on the beds, I on the floor at Father D.'s feet—and listened to the word of God.

Gradually, while living in his brother's house, Father D. was saving money to buy a piece of land adjacent to the farm where he'd been brought up. He'd never talked about his childhood, but that wasn't unusual; we weren't used to thinking of priests as having had a childhood, but it was clear it was important to him to reclaim his father's land. Once, when he took us to see a pond that was almost entirely weed choked and covered with a film of algae, he showed us a picture of him and his brothers standing there fifty years before, five naked boys, lined up in size order, their heads shaved. Everyone else seemed to think this was funny, but I was terrified. It was, among other things, my first photograph of the male nude.

After he'd made the purchase, we'd take picnics to the land, and pretend to think it was beautiful. It had no distinguishing features: ruined fields, a distant view of unremarkable hills, scrub pines, and plain, ungiving oaks. He rented space on the end to a man who worked as an orderly at the hospital where Father D. was the fill-in chaplain. The man parked a trailer on his rented space. One day he brought home a wife, equally obese, equally silent.

Then there was a child. But we never spoke more than a greeting to any of them. When her mother died, one of the women from the working women's retreat group gave Father D. the money she'd been left to build himself a house, and next to it, one for her and her sister. This caused great consternation among the other women; did their proximity constitute a scandal? Really, they were horribly jealous. He built his house himself, as cheaply as he could; it was made of cinder blocks; it was only one floor and it had the punishing lack of adornment of a barracks. The woman who'd provided the money was eager to move in and hired a builder to do the house for her and her sister; it, too, was one story, plain but in a way that suggested the estate of spinsterhood rather than, like his, a court-martial.

Her sister had a heart attack and died before she could move in. When we visited, we were invited to stay with the living sister, but we didn't. We slept at the motel and came to Father D.'s house during the day, where he would hold forth while we listened. I was beginning to fancy myself a Romantic poet and took myself for walks. But there was nothing to look at and when I think of those walks, all I remember is dry burdocks sticking like car-buncles to my jeans, wounding my fingers when I tried to pull them off. But while I welcomed the walks, I was beginning to be bored by Father D.'s obsessive rants about the badness of the world; I was beginning to enjoy the world, and suspected that he might be missing some-thing.

★   ★   ★

The last time I was there, Father D. and I had a fight about Daniel Berrigan. Father Berrigan had poured blood over draft records, been hunted by the FBI, and gone to jail. Father D. said he was a traitor; I said he was a hero. Father D. slammed his whiskey glass down onto the wooden refectory table. "Get out of my house," he said.

I heard the doom in that sentence; I was not only being disowned, I was being excommunicated. But I stubbornly obeyed. It was ten at night. But I obeyed, and walked into the anonymous night. One of my mother's friends came after me in the car. We went back to the motel; Father D. had gone to bed. In the morning, the last day of our visit, we returned and nothing was said. Father D. tried to joke with me, and, as he always did, he wept when we kissed good-bye. But that time I was unmoved. I knew I wouldn't come back again, and I never did. Two years later he was dead.

By the time of his death, I was married, living with my first husband in my own house. Two years earlier, I would have felt bereft by his death, but when he died I felt primarily relief. There were no priests in my life, no pilgrimages I would have to make to hear them speak, to share their company, to bask in their presence. In my new house, there were no white linen towels set apart for the priests' anointed hands. If somehow I met a priest somewhere whom I might be tempted to invite for a meal, I'd think the better of it. I would remember that my husband thought the Church was superstitious mumbo jumbo and that any welcome he would give a priest would be, at best, only partial, granted equivocally, and only for my sake. And then later, I would be judged for my weakness, my sentimentality. It wouldn't be worth it. The way that I was living, the man I had chosen to live with, made it necessary that there would be no priests in my house.

∞∞∞∞∞∞∞∞∞∞∞

In 1959, when I was ten, a newly ordained priest was assigned to our parish. A special romance attached to newly ordained priests. They were so young, scarcely out of boyhood, scarcely out of their mothers' homes or arms, and yet they held our eternal life in their hands. Watching them from the rear—which was the way you saw them most of the time, since in those days priests faced the altar, not the congregation to say Mass—you could see, grazing their vestments, the boyish declivities of the backs of their necks. You ached for them each time they got a haircut.

That year, Father W. must have been twenty-four. I remember coming upon him in church when he, like me, was "making a visit," the term that was used for off-hour praying—before the Blessed Sacrament. He knelt with his head bent, his hands pressed lightly together as if he were squeezing something between them. Occasionally, he would lift his head, but he kept his eyes squeezed tightly shut. He seemed to be in some sort of spiritual anguish, for which I envied him, and honored. I knew that he had no idea I was there, and I was humbled by such a thorough absorption. When I prayed, there was always one part of me that watched what everyone around me thought of this image of a girl in prayer. I knew there was no part of Father W. that watched himself.

Young priests like Father W. would do anything for the parish: coach CYO (Catholic Youth Organization) basketball, train the altar boys, moderate the Rosary Society, make house calls at all hours. And this was why he was in our house, in an official capacity, unlike the other priests I'd seen walking through the door. He came in silence, carrying Viaticum. Each week he brought Communion to my dying grandmother.

In 1961, my grandmother got sick. Her colon was removed and she returned home from the hospital with a colostomy; we were told she had less than a year to live.

She lay in her bed, silent, and stunned. Like a child, she had to be changed several times a day. The smell of the shit that came out of the hole in her stomach permeated the house, and I was never free of it. She had a series of small strokes that affected her ability to swallow, so a suction machine was installed to pull the phlegm from her throat so that she wouldn't choke. I felt as if I was watching a giant tree rot steadily from the blight that spread inside her, a blight whose manifestation I could see: the red, raw bump on her stomach that had to be kept scrupulously clean.

Her archaic and iconic bedroom was transformed into an ordinary sickroom. Her bed with its iron bedstead was removed and a hospital bed with bars and pulleys took its place; a series of tin tables with wheels replaced her wardrobe; they were covered with gauze and cotton and Vaseline and bottles of medicine, liquid and pills.

Her smell, and the constant gurgling in her throat overpowered me. They were the atmosphere in which I lived, I had to give in to them, take them into my own body, I was saturated in them, they were too powerful for me to escape or to avoid. This was the atmosphere into which Father W. walked each Saturday, his young hair still damp from the shower, the smell of a too-close shave still on him, male and healthy: Noxzema, Old Spice. He entered the atmosphere of the house like a scalpel cutting through diseased tissue. I almost didn't want him coming into our house, entering the stench and the heavy air of female decay. At the same time, his immaculate young maleness seemed to redeem and purify the air, which sometimes to me was literally unbreathable. When he walked in the door, his eyes lowered, the purple stole around his neck, reaching into his black pocket for the pyx that held the Host, I felt a lightening of atmosphere that made me think there was some hope for my future life. But I was afraid for him: what was he giving up, bestowing this lightness upon us? What poison was he taking in?

He removed, by his presence, the tincture of death. But only temporarily. When he left, taking with him the gold pyx, now empty, that had held the Host that now resided in my grandmother's cancerous insides, the disease took over once again. We were the tenants of the estate not only of death, but of dying. My grandmother lost the power of speech, so she would look at me with eyes that were imploring first, then furious if she wasn't under-stood. Every moment I was near her, I wanted only to run away as fast, as violently as I could. But I knew the saints would not have run away. I offered my terror to God, knowing you could offer anything to God, even your most unworthy temptations, so long as you didn't succumb, and he would glorify them.

My mother and my aunt felt I should be taught to change my grandmother's colostomy and to use the suction machine. As the months went on, they asked me to tend her more and more frequently. Retching, I would dip rags into the blue tin basin by her bed. I undid the colostomy's complicated bandage with its twelve interlocking tails. I washed around her bump, then disinfected it. I rubbed Vaseline on her stomach and covered the area in gauze. I took a new bandage from the pile of clean ones and rebandaged her, weaving the tails securely so that there would be no leaks. It didn't occur to me to ask if I could be spared these jobs. If I didn't do them, everything fell to my mother and my aunt. And they were crippled; I was able bodied, whole.

Only Father W. seemed to notice that I had too much responsibility for a twelve year old. He asked my mother and my aunt if they thought it was right for me to be doing so much. My mother looked away from him, but my aunt stared him right down. "It's her grandmother, she loves her," my aunt said, in the tight voice no one could counter. Father W. gave up. I was glad he did; I knew he couldn't win, and an unsuccessful battle waged on my part would have been more demoralizing than a timely retreat.

He would try to speak to me when he came to bring my grandmother Communion. But he was shy with girls, and I felt unworthy of his attention, so I was tongue-tied in his presence. Before that, I had nothing to do with him, except the time I watched him in prayer. He was always with the boys, taking them to the beach or playing furious ball games. And I wouldn't have dreamed of going to Confession to him. I didn't want to stain his purity with the defilement of my constant sin.

After he'd given my grandmother Communion, and returned the gold pyx to his pocket, my mother and my aunt buzzed around him, offering him food (which, unlike the other priests that came to the house, he never took), trying to get him to talk about sports the way they had with their silent brothers. But he always seemed eager to be on his way. "You know where to find me, any hour of the day or night," he said, and they believed him. I don't know what I believed.

It was he who married my aunt to the man who'd darkened the weekends of my preadolescence, in the time when there was still a semblance of youthfulness to my life, the time before my grandmother's illness. This was the wedding I happened upon during a class trip. He'd performed the marriage, then come to our house to break the news to my mother. When I got home, Father W. was comforting my mother, his arm around her while she wept. "How could she do this to me now? How can she leave me all alone with my mother in that state?" I don't know what he said. Perhaps he said that God would take care of everything.

Some weeks later, at the end of June, my mother and I went to Staten Island to visit friends for a weekend. My mother had had full charge of my grandmother for a month and a half. She was exhausted. Father W. told her she needed to get away. At eleven o'clock the night we arrived, the phone rang. It was my newly married aunt, who'd agreed to take care of my grandmother for the weekend, saying my grandmother had just died.

My mother wept like an animal, in a way that made no place for any of the living. Our friends had to drive us home. When we entered the house, she began howling. I knew nothing would make her stop. She was alone with her dead mother, and she didn't care who saw her grief. I wanted to shake her, to strike her, to make her silent, above all to keep my aunt from seeing her like this. But she had no impulse to cover herself. My aunt regarded her wailing contemptuously. My mother said, "It makes me sick to think that he was the one to close my mother's eyes." My aunt had been quick to tell everyone that her husband should have that last privilege, that she felt my grandmother's choosing to die when they were there was a blessing on her new marriage.

My mother raged and howled; my aunt received her sisters and brothers calmly, at the center of the house, clothed in the blessing she had stolen. No one wanted to look at my mother. I stood by her, trying to quiet her. But nothing I did mattered. Only when Father W. came into the house and spoke to her alone did she quiet down.

He buried my grandmother and tried to make peace between my mother and my aunt. But he wasn't strong enough. He couldn't order them to behave differently, as another priest might have done, under pain of mortal sin. Gently, like the boy he was, he urged them to try to love each other as Christ had loved them. They didn't listen to a word he said.

One Saturday during the summer after my grandmother's death, I went to church at the time for Confession, knowing I was in a state of mortal sin. Usually, there were five priests hearing Confession, and I switched around so no priest would become too familiar with me. My first choice was usually the pastor, who was a little deaf and too busy with administrative work to know the parish children. But I didn't even take a chance with him. I kept moving. In doing this, I denied myself the luxury of one confessor, but that was a luxury and not a rule, and since it was only myself I denied, I chose deprivation over embarrassment.

But that hot August day, everyone else must have been on vacation. Only Father W. was hearing confessions. When I understood this, I was sickened by my lack of choice. To go on longer than I had to in a state of mortal sin because of something so paltry as psychological discomfort would have been a serious error, perhaps even sinful in itself. I knew without question that nothing like my own personal happiness was a factor in a decision such as this. I had to enter the confessional, there was no other way.

It was the only time I remember the body of a priest giving off any odor at all. It was a high, thin smell, suggesting not dirt, but anxiety. The closed space of the confessional—a wooden closet ventilated only by the holes in the screens between confessor and penitent—was the perfect cave for the breeding of dread.

The screen between us was an accordion-shaped, plastic, amber-colored one, with little air holes punched through. I hoped for a minute that he'd say he couldn't go on, it was just too hot in there, but I knew that wouldn't happen. I wanted to spare him the offensiveness of my sin; I thought he was too pure to have to hear it. But I was well versed in sacramental lore; I knew that, really, it didn't matter what priest was performing the sacrament, the sacrament itself was sufficiently potent to wipe out the accident of personality. *Ex opere operans,* I kept saying to myself, repeating the words that expressed the principle: it is not the worker that matters, but the work.

I offered my mortification to the Lord. I confessed my "private impurity," wanting only to be out of the dark box, out in the light of the church where I could be exalted.

"You shouldn't worry about things like that. What you did is nothing to worry about," Father W. said.

I felt ill, as if someone had told me the law of gravity no longer applied. I felt myself falling, heels over head, tumbling into an endless darkness. I wanted to run away from the confessional, and go somewhere else, live some other way, speak to someone who made sense, whose words I could make sense of, and live by.

"Think of the boundless love of God and try to love others as you have been loved. And go in peace."

It was as if he'd demolished the walls of the confessional, leaving me, an animal whose habitat had been the lightless cellar, suddenly exposed to light, a light which hurt my eyes and rendered everything they fell on entirely unrecognizable.

For the first time, I felt no exaltation kneeling at the altar saying my penance. I was horribly afraid. Nothing in life had prepared me to believe that the sin that had tormented me for years was just a phantom. The overlarge, newly built church, which I had never liked but which usually seemed, after I left the confessional, to be a miracle of airiness, now seemed only vacant and unmarked. I said my prayers perfunctorily. I thought for a moment that perhaps Father W. had lost his mind. You read about things like that, and the questions arose in that case whether the practitioner's incapacity made the sacrament invalid. I considered asking my mother to drive me to another parish to confess again.

I walked and walked in the heavy heat, passing the familiar stores; the pharmacy, the luncheonette, the medical supply store with its trusses, bedpans, crutches that I always felt I couldn't pass without a proper look. As I walked, I began to consider the possibility that Father W. was right. Things began to look different. The lettering on the store signs began to come into focus. I went into a soda fountain and had a lemon ice-cream soda: it was cool and fresh, and made my tongue feel cleansed. As I walked into the street, the faces of the people whom I saw moved me by their acuteness. The sound of a car door shutting, a dog's bark, seemed to me sharp and true like music. I thought of the blind man whom Jesus cured, who said that men seemed to him at first like trees walking. I was walking like that, in space that seemed newly familiar to me. I had to try, on my own, to imagine how to live in the new way Father W. suggested that I could. Try and make friends, he said. People your own age. Have fun for a change.

But how could I live like that in the house where my grandmother had just died? I knew then that I would have to leave the house, that I would have to leave the church, because to live with this new sense of lightness and clarity I would need a dwelling that let in the light.

Nearly twenty years later, when my first book was published, someone named W. phoned me up. At first, I didn't recognize the name. I knew that he'd left the priesthood to marry, but I didn't know what happened after that: the shame of his defection had turned him anonymous, an exile, a betrayer. He said he was so proud of me, so happy for my success. He told me he was living on the eastern end of Long Island, that he was a social worker, his wife was a psychologist, they had two little girls. He invited me to his house for a barbecue.

I said yes, but I never showed up. I didn't want to visit him in an ordinary house; I didn't want him cooking meat for me over charcoal, wearing a funny apron and a funny hat. He was a priest forever, according to the order of Melchisadech. I understood that he had given me a freedom I denied to him but there was nothing I could do about the failure of my heart. He was a feature of the architecture of the past: formal, restricted, public, grand. I

didn't want to think of him inhabiting a dwelling consecrated to nothing more than ordinary human happiness. I
didn't want to think of him having a home. I didn't want
to think of any priest having a home, and I didn't want to
think of him as anything other than a priest. I needed
priests to be heroic so that I could place myself heroically
in relation to them, away from the fixed lot of women,
with their ordinary fate of hearth and home.

If a priest was a man, like any other, with a home like
anybody else's, he was emptied of potential to transform
the places where he'd rest, impermanently, his anointed
head. And these transformations were the only ones I
could imagine myself a part of. So I, too, would be
deprived of transformation. The food I ate and served, the
linens that I washed and ironed, would have no resonance
with the Last Supper or residue of the sacred Host. No
house I lived in would lodge in its walls the hint of matter turned to spirit or eternal life. Everything connected
to me would be, hopelessly and always, only what it was.

SANCTUARY
IN A
CITY OF DISPLAY

MY FIRST VISION of Rome was an image of Saint Peter's, seen through the lens of something called a View-Master, which looked a bit like a camera, a bit like binoculars, a bit like a diving mask. It was brown plastic with two cloudy plastic lenses in the front and a slit in the top into which was put a disc with pie-shaped slices of film separated from one another by white cardboard. You looked into the back of the View-Master and saw an image in three dimensions. Then you flicked a lever on the side and the image changed. I owned four series of discs. One was called "California, Land of Sunshine." One was called simply "Disneyland." The other two, befitting my family's religious seriousness, were "The Passion Plays of Oberammergau," and "The Vatican."

Frozen, utterly complete in their unnaturalness, the images I saw seemed more possessed of information than what the eye could take in or the mind contain. Since the vision was entirely private, what was conveyed had the crucial significance of a whispered conversation, the life or death quality of an encoded message from a spymaster to a spy. The images seemed embedded in an unbreakable eternal silence; no movement would stir the air. It wasn't clear to me whether the figures I beheld were alive or dead, had ever been alive, or were made of wax. Jesus carrying his cross, crowned with thorns, kneeling in agony in the Garden of Olives; the pope in his tiered, elaborate biretta, raising his hand in blessing; the orange growers on the ladders in their groves—were these actors, or dolls, or the humans they claimed to be?

With the contraption held against my eyes, I was plunged into an atmosphere of equivocal artificiality. Why did I love it so? Did I feel, looking at their false dimensionality, their vividness which could not have come from life, that I was entering into ultimate danger, where I, too, could be rendered unalive or static, or ultimate safety, where all the dangers of the world could be, at the flick of a lever, neutralized into paralysis, the joke potency of dream?

I loved the silence of those images, their freedom, not only from noise but from the harsh demands of time. Because nothing was alive, nothing would change. Having partaken so entirely of death they were entirely free of death's surprises. But I wasn't, of course, thinking of death when I put the mask up to my eyes. If you asked me what I liked, I would have said, "The colors."

When I inserted the disc called "The Vatican," the pale face of the pope emerged from a matte background of rose red. His hive-shaped papal hat, embroidered gold and white, dwarfed his refined skull. His ring seemed, in the same way, too big for his fingers. His gaze met nothing, the blessing indicated by his raised hand could fall on no living head. In the next frame, Saint Peter's, looking thousands of times more important than the Capitol, pressed itself, gray and essential, against a silver sky where no birds flew. On the ground, ant-size priests in birettas walked, holding breviaries. There must have been a picture of the Sistine Chapel, but I don't remember it. Only the white face of the pope, his rimless spectacles, the gray dome of Saint Peter's, the gray expanse of the square where priests in black read their black books.

And they would never change. Rules would come from these men, from the huge dome, from the gold throne on which the pope sat with his permanently upraised finger. Words would be spoken that were a part of universal truth. *Ex cathedra*. Words removed from the possibility of emendation and of argument. Words rising up from silence, which I, in my privileged position as a Catholic, had only to obey.

I did not imagine that the pope, the cardinals, or the priests spoke to one another, or if they ever spoke, it was in anything but Latin. Not for them the colorful, playful, songlike or outraged Italian of my downstairs neighbors, from whose apartment the smell of strong coffee, roasting nuts, simmering sauces, would waft through our floors. When I thought of Rome, I did not think of Italy, nor did I think of it as a place where anyone like myself might go. My being there was of no importance to my thoughts about the place. I did not contemplate a contemporary city resembling New York, any more than I had images of empire. Rome was the Church, the Vatican. The Vatican had nothing to do with a living people, a living city. Like the images I looked through, it was frozen. The Eternal City. But I knew it was its own country, a state unto itself, outside of ordinary law. At the center of the Vatican, clothed in white, entirely self-contained, his rimless glasses glinting, his cultivated hands raised in blessing, was the pope. Pius XII.

I believed that beneath the place where the pope's throne was fixed lay the bodies of the early Christian martyrs in their catacombs. So soon after the word *Rome* came to my mind, it was followed by the name of the pope, and then the names of the Christian martyrs: Agnes, Cecilia, Anastasia, Perpetua, Agatha, Lucy.

I was quite afraid of being martyred. Or rather I was afraid of being given the test (I would have said then the privilege) of martyrdom, and failing. In the years I speak of—1953 to '58—the years between my first memories and the death of Pius XII, martyrs were on our minds again because we believed a new crop of them was being, as we spoke, raised up. These were martyrs to communism, and I feared a Russian soldier holding a gun to my throat as I imagined the virgin martyrs feared the Roman soldiers with their helmets and sinewy naked legs and swords. Would I have the strength, as they had, to withstand?

Many of the Roman martyrs whom I fixed on were women. And often, in their case, though not in the case of the males, the word *martyr* was preceded by the word *vir-*.

gin. It would be many years before I would understand the literal meaning of the word *virgin,* so innocent was I of the details of sex. For a long time, I thought the word was a synonym for unmarried.

Each day at Mass we said their names. Each met her death in Rome: a sword through her breast, beheaded, her eyes plucked out, or devoured by lions. I saw, without knowing it, the imperial light of Rome in them; for they were wealthy Roman women, many of them, and when I imagined them, they stood in high rooms, empty of furniture, except for one chair and a couch for their reclining. The young women raised their hands in supplication or in blessing. Or they stood, hands at their sides, and let the lions rush at them. If they were rushed at by lions, they must have been in the Coliseum, but I didn't see the Coliseum walls, only the open ground where women stood, surrounded by invisible cheering crowds. They shed their blood under a cloudless sky, so bright after their underground life, the life of the catacombs, the same light where the Jewish children hid during the war, the same light in which I lived in terror of being forced to hide.

The virgin martyrs wore sandals, they walked on marble floors, they ate olives and flat bread. They suffered torments and violations. They stood in silver light or were suffused in darkness. They gave everything.

I saw their pictures in the lives of the saints or on the holy cards I was given as rewards or prizes. They carried their symbols, a palm, a lamb, a plate holding eyes. They both terrified me and caused me shame, because my shallow spirit prayed to be spared their fate and I was told I ought to be praying for the opposite.

From the ground drenched by their shed blood sprang up the dome of Saint Peter's, different from any building on the surface of the earth.

ooooooooooooooo

My first hint that there was a city that existed at the same time as my own life came to me from the very first film I was taken to see: *Three Coins in the Fountain.* Why my parents chose this as my first film, rather than some wholesome children's picture, something by Disney, something about animals or fairy-tale creatures, is a question I can't answer.

Three Coins in the Fountain was not an entirely appropriate film to take a five year old to see. It was about three American women—now we would say women but it is more faithful to the spirit of the film to say it was about three American girls. The youngest, played by Maggie McNamara, who in real life died soon afterward, is a typical Midwestern naive. The middle one (played by Jean Peters, married in real life to Howard Hughes, who stopped her career out of jealousy) is voluptuous and good-natured and down to earth. She's going home, telling her employers, for no reason that makes any possible narrative sense, that she's about to be married. She's really going home because she believes it's impossible for an American girl to find a husband in Rome.

The third, older and wiser, is played by Dorothy McGuire, of whose real life I have no knowledge. At the beginning of the film she has been, for fifteen years, the indispensable secretary of a famous American writer played by Clifton Webb. She is secretly in love with him, as Jean Peters is secretly in love with Rossano Brazzi, who works with her and is secretly in love with *her.* But neither of them can reveal their love because of the company rule against employee dating. Maggie McNamara is secretly in love with an Italian prince, played by that famous Italian, Louis Jourdan.

Through a series of shenanigans all three girls end up in the arms of the men they love at the fountain of Trevi. What did I take away from this film, one of the first in Technicolor? Images of great buildings, of fountains and flowers, of people singing, of women in beautiful dresses with tight waists and full skirts, wearing high heels and small hats, or straw hats and sandals laced halfway up the calf. Never mind: it was style and good fortune that I understood, and the idea that love came to the ardent, the audacious, and the patient, against a background of delightfully splashing water wetting the marble skins of indolent, reclining gods.

Against the same background, but more elegant and more heartbreaking, stood Audrey Hepburn in *Roman Holiday.* I never saw it in a theater, but I watched it at least once a year on the "Late Show," weeping with my mother or one of my girlfriends. From this film, I learned that Rome was the place that allowed you a respite from good behavior, a day off from duty, that you could get your hair cut and eat a gelato and ride on a Vespa and drink champagne at an outdoor cafe which I did not know was on

Piazza del Popolo, only that it seemed like a place where I could be happy, with a carefreeness open to me nowhere else. Watching Audrey Hepburn and Gregory Peck, I believed that you could kiss and be kissed, offering everything, but only temporarily. I could become a princess, a pretty girl, a girl who gave up love for responsibility, but not yet. It was the not yet that Rome offered me; the not yet that I dreamed of traveling to.

But there was another side of Rome, a darker side that my friends and I discovered in 1965 when we snuck into the city and found the Thalia, a theater on Ninety-sixth and Broadway that showed old movies, to see a film we had been expressly forbidden to see, a film that had been on the Legion of Decency condemned list for at least five years. This was the Rome of sin and decadence: *La Dolce Vita*.

It opens, even, with a joke against the Church, the pope. A statue of Jesus hangs from a helicopter like Fay Wray from King Kong's hand. The bathing beauties on the roof ask, in their bikinis, where Jesus is going. Pantomiming from a helicopter, Marcello Mastroianni tells them it is going to the pope.

So it was possible to make fun of the Church, the pope, and not be struck down. Only placed on the condemned list, which by 1965 even some priests were ignoring. They wrote articles, for which other priests attacked them, talking about the theme of Redemption in *La Dolce Vita*. But my friends and I did not see Redemption: we saw elegance and sophistication. We tried to imagine ourselves looking like Anouk Aiméle in a little black dress. We wondered how she could drive at night in sun-glasses. We were afraid of what we would say to Marcello Mastroianni; we wondered if, with us, he would no longer be bored. We imagined ourselves talking about how bored we were over drinks at cafes on the Via Veneto, but we couldn't imagine how anyone could be bored in such a place. With a terrible sense of inadequacy which we imagined would be cured only by European travel, we contemplated replacing an ideal of goodness with one of knowingness, a dream of being beloved with a dream of sophistication. We yearned for the possibility of never being surprised, therefore never being made to look foolish. We thought this might happen to us if we rode in Alfa Romeo convertibles and had enough sex so that it no longer seemed extraordinary. And then, perhaps, like the world-weary party goers, we would be truly and dependably wise.

The first time I traveled to Europe, I didn't visit Rome. It was 1971, I was twenty-two; I had a knapsack on my back. It had taken me two years to save the five hundred dollars that would allow me to stay in Europe for ten weeks. I went to Florence where I fell in love with a vacuum cleaner salesman named Giuseppe whom I met on the Piazalle Michelangelo. *Ay-lay-tro-loo* was the way he pronounced the product that he sold, the famous Electrolux. Electro*lux* I would say, trying to coach him in the single bed of his pensione, on the double bed of his brother's house where we would go on Sundays while they picnicked in the country. But he couldn't pronounce that final *x*, any more than I could remember to make the number of my Italian verbs agree with my Italian subjects. I lived with him for a month instead of going to Rome.

So I came to Rome for the first time five years later with my mother and my first husband, miserably married. The trip had nothing to do with anything I had seen in the movies; it had much more to do with martyrdom. My mother and my husband didn't like each other and it was her first time in a non–English-speaking country. I was the only one with any Italian. My mother wanted only to see the pope; my husband, naturally, wanted to see the ancient sites and eat in restaurants. I was always on the verge of tears.

Because of my mother, I learned the Italian word for wheelchair, *sedia a rotelle,* and, heart in my mouth, contemplated pushing her across the pathological Roman streets. But she didn't like being on the street. She was panicked by the traffic, by the foreign words buzzing around her, uttered by the quick-moving pedestrians. She wouldn't leave her room in the pensione found for her by a priest she knew in New York. Or, no—that's not precisely true, we left twice. Once, to visit a priest who was a friend of the priest who had found her her pensione in his monastery off the Appian Way. We sat with this priest, a quiet man of Pittsburgh, and drank tea. We left after half an hour. The next day we went to a papal Mass at Saint Peter's, and because she was in a wheelchair, my mother was shown to a spot near the altar. The pope blessed her as he walked out. All she could say afterward, over and over, like a trauma victim, or one who has seen the face of God and lived, was, "He smelled like raisins. He smelled just like raisins."

I spent my days playing cards with my mother on the bed in her room in the pensione. The ceilings were ornamented and extravagant, like the ceilings in the Vatican; I had a view of the Roman roofs. But these were my only sights. Because my mother was crippled, the owners and the chambermaids of the pensione were indulgent and understanding and kind. They allowed her to take all her meals in her room. I left her only to buy rolls, cheese, and tomatoes; at night, my husband and I, in the room next to hers, fought in dry, tight whispers. After he fell asleep, I wept.

The first time I came to Rome by myself it was to interview Natalia Ginzburg, an Italian writer whom I much admired and whom I believed was underappreciated by American audiences. I came to Ginzburg not through the sacred images of my childhood or the overlarge ones of films, but through reading. I was entirely grown up by the time that I read about Rome, before I realized that Rome had had a nineteenth century, and more important, a Second World War, which I had thought of happening only in Germany and France.

It must have been the example of Henry James and his characters that led me to pursue Ginzburg in the way I did. I approached Ginzburg via Moravia and Pavese, but in my thoughts about her there was a touch of appetite for the complicated unhappiness of *La Dolce Vita*. Like any Jamesian innocent, I came reverent, in awe of the distinguished older woman who had lost her husband in a Fascist prison, who had lived underground with her children, who had been the only woman not married to a successful man among the band of postwar Italian writers, who had lost another husband, and had a brain-damaged child. I was visiting European suffering; I would arrive, a pilgrim, on my knees.

Months ahead of time, I had written to make an appointment to interview her. She had written back to confirm the date. When I arrived, jet-lagged but full of excitement, having flown across the ocean precisely to see her, she said she was too busy. She was a member of Parliament and that day she was *in camera*. I was terribly disappointed. I called the friend of an English friend, a woman who had known Ginzburg for years. I didn't know that this is the only way things are done in Italy: through some kind of private familial or quasi-familial arrangement. At least, an inside connection. The friend of my friend spoke to Ginzburg who agreed to see me in four days. I was in Rome, alone, with nothing to do but explore the city.

It was one of those periods of borderless, nourishing solitude. I had no expectations. I had only one plan: to stay away from the Vatican. The dome of Saint Peter's seemed to me a bully presence, and the overornamented huge interior was a monument, not to the spirit, but to the pomp and force of the Church of Rome, the part of Catholicism I keep trying to forget. I did the simplest thing I could think of, something unlike myself. I permitted myself to wander the streets, allowing my eyes to fall and rest on whatever pleased them. I could only allow myself to do this alone, because Rome is a very easy city to get lost in and when I am lost with other people, most particularly a man, I feel simultaneously enraged that they have been so irresponsible as to get us lost, and at the same time ashamed with a shame that is literally paralyzing. I stand still in the middle of a street and cannot move because no place seems as if it wouldn't be tainted by the presence of a person who has allowed herself (and others with her) to get lost.

But when I'm alone, I really don't mind getting lost because there's no one to be ashamed in front of. I can find my own debility amusing, even interesting, leading to some hidden good fortune I could not have planned, or, if nothing else, to some future funny stories. And at first, I didn't get lost; I was very proud of myself for being able, with no wrong turnings, to get from Campo dei Fiori to Piazza Navona.

It was January but the sun blazed and it was warm enough to eat outdoors. The piazza was still tarted up for Christmas. The shops and restaurants were festooned with tinsel. It was the day before the Feast of the Kings and everyone was out for the *passeggiata*. Someone was playing "I Get Ideas" on an accordion. An antique carousel, set up for children to ride on, spun, empty, in the center of the square. Its pastel horses with floral bridles brought to mind Nellie Melba, Jenny Lind. Chinese lanterns that ought to have looked cheap but didn't swung in the breeze. Six men dressed as medieval peasants did some sort of traditional dance, playing wooden pipes, wearing shoes made of straw that laced up their calves, like the girls in *Three Coins in the Fountain*. A beggar woman carried a sign around her neck: I AM A POOR GRAND-MOTHER. How had this happened in Italy, this failure of family? Even in its failure, though, it was the family that was invoked. The Bernini statues gestured to a sky with a few thick clouds through which the sun shot down in slanted rays: the source of the Baroque.

I allowed myself simply to enjoy everything I saw and smelled and heard and tasted; I allowed myself to make mistakes in grammar, to apologize, and to go on. Why not? There was, on the Roman streets, not one suggestion of punishment or shame. If there were shadows, my eyes did not fall on them; the narrow streets held no dangers for me, only curiosities, only perhaps an old dish in a shop window, a bakery, a shoemaker. The sun warmed the white or yellow stones, enlivened the water in the fountains. The blare of the horns was absorbed in sunlight, the shouts on the streets would lead to no recriminations. If this city had been the home of persecutions, that was long ago, and those people had been replaced by a new race that was devoted not to the conquest of empire, but to *la bella figura:* the ideal that things should look good and one should always be turned out well. That things should be seen, and therefore be pleasing to the eye. This was not a people of helmets and swords, constructors of aqueducts and systems of law; allowances would be made on these streets by the people who lived on them. That meant allowances would be made for me.

★   ★   ★

My humility about my own weak sense of direction returned to me when I tried to find the church of Santa Maria in Trastevere. I kept asking directions, but I am bad at following directions, particularly in Italian, and once across the Tiber, wherever I turned, I seemed to be walking toward Saint Peter's Square.

Finally, I gave in and walked into the square. It was comparatively empty, except for a huge crown of Asian nuns in short gray coats and white veils. A Swiss guard looked silly in glasses. Silly, too, perched high up on a platform at the top of the staircase, was a Christmas tree, which I reckoned must be bigger than the one in Rockefeller Center. But whereas the New York tree gave me a sense that all was right with the world, this one looked apologetic, a false gesture made inexpertly—a bow toward the domestic—and the domestic and the inexpert are exactly what it is the greatness of Saint Peter's not to touch.

I entered the basilica thinking of Ezra Pound's idea of the perfect image, "That the child should walk at peace in the basilica, the light there almost solid." But nothing merely narrative could be set here, except perhaps the impersonal narrative of unquestioned power. And a child, if we are not brutes, must be seen as always narrative and always personal. So Pound's image, in seeming impossible, grew newly intriguing to me. Standing in the basilica where what he spoke of would not have happened, the image became something else I could not believe in. I passed by the Pietà, which like the Mona Lisa can no longer properly be looked at. It reminds me only of copies of itself, and of the 1964 World's Fair, where I went with my girlfriends and tried to meet boys.

I passed statues of popes who look like ancient Romans and saints who look like the Statue of Liberty. I was moved by Bernini's *Holy Spirit,* but not nearly so much as I was by his Saint Teresa, which says something to me about the life of the spirit, which this place does not any more than the Teddy Roosevelt rotunda in the Museum of Natural History says something to me about nature. Both were about mastery; both created in me a desire for hopeless rebellion, in which I knew I'd be crushed.

Only downstairs in Saint Peter's by the tomb of the popes, particularly of Pope John XXIII, did I find the spirit of devotion missing for me in the Grand Basilica. There was a bouquet of fresh flowers in front of Pope John's tomb and I knelt there, feeling quieter than I had since I got to Rome.

Perhaps it was that quiet, or the flexible spirit of Pope John, that allowed me to find my way to the Church of Santa Cecilia. She was one of the martyrs of my childhood, but this church erased the terror of her fate.

Although it commemorated the vicious beheading of an innocent and musical matron, it did not call to mind blood or hacking swords: the memorial was not accomplished by mimesis. In the courtyard there was a Roman urn filled with dark pink roses, a fountain, a place to sit, to rest, to look at the eighteenth-century facade, the twelfth-century portico, the Roman columns. Here, in front of me, was all of history, and nothing was dangerous. There was no compulsion. Sit, rest, listen to the splash of water, let your eye fall on the color of the roses. Inside the church, the statue of Saint Cecilia recalled not her beheading, but her body having been found intact hundreds of years later, a beautiful woman in a golden gown. The reclining statue of her, by the seventeenth-century sculptor Maderno, reminded me of the statue on One Hundred Sixth Street and Broadway. A memorial to those who went down with the *Titanic*.

Cecilia is a prosperous, slumbering matron, over-taken—but gracefully rather than brutally—by a tragic fate. Her face is invisible; it is turned down on the marble slab on which she rests, but her body is slanted toward us. The veil, or turban, which wraps her head spreads out languorously from her body, which we cannot believe dead, only sleeping. In death, she is not only peaceful, but fashionable. There is nothing to be feared.

And if, that night, when I walked alone behind the Pantheon, in the Piazza Farnese, on the Via Giulia, with its churches whose facades sport embedded stone skulls, I could imagine the crushing hoof of imperial or ecclesiastical power, I knew there would be nothing personal in the force that might destroy whatever came in its path. It would annihilate; but it would not humiliate. The terror would be only physical, not moral, not spiritual. There would be no shame.

In the morning, the streets would be cleaned; water would splash, and a block from the Piazza Farnese, the Via

Giulia, in the Campo Dei Fiori, fruits and cheese would be, once again, beautifully for sale. Light, color, movement, would once more do their work. The city, I discovered, was nothing like what I had seen in the View-Master. The death that was invoked in this city was a drama, like Caravaggio's *Crucifixion of Saint Peter* or *Execution of Saint Matthew.* It was not the terrifying end of motion; not an eternal freeze-frame. The death that Rome insists we not forget is simply an afterthought, the last chapter of a story which is, after all, called life. The life of Bernini's figures, whose dramatic gestures are from the same lexicon as Caravaggio's: the lexicon of endless movement, endless change. This is not a lesson that I learned as a child, when I imagined Rome, alone in my room, with my solitary visions; it was a lesson I knew I would have to relearn each time I came back (and I vowed that I would come back again and again), and could relearn, as long as I kept my back turned on the Vatican.

After four days of wandering and musing, it was time to meet with Natalia Ginzburg. She was not warm; she was *stretta,* severe leaning toward dry. As the word suggests, she was impressed by my devotion, but she was impatient with my questions about her as a woman writer. She wanted to talk about politics, Italian politics, which I knew nothing about. Occasionally, I could hear a terrible guttural cry from upstairs, and then a nurse would run upstairs and the cries were silenced. Ginzburg said nothing about this and I pretended not to notice, understanding that it was the brain-damaged daughter.

She agreed, at my Italian friend's invitation, to have dinner with me the next evening. We had a moment of communication when we both recalled being teenage girls reading the Russian novelists and feeling that we had finally learned the truth and that because of this, the world would open before us. I began dreaming: I would come back again and again. She would ask me to stay in her huge apartment in Vecchia Roma. She would say, "You are my heir, my daughter." She would say, "I didn't expect so much from an American."

None of this happened. Instead, like a Jamesian character, I was made to do something I didn't want to do, something against my values, something I knew was wrong. She asked that I show her what I was going to write before I published it. This was entirely unprofessional and I should have answered coolly, "Mi dispiace, ma non è possibile."

But how could I? She was the real thing, the real European writer who had suffered in the war. Suffered as no American, no one of my generation had. How could I say no to my literary mother? I'd had a hard enough time saying no to my real mother. Fifteen years earlier, I hadn't even been able to get her out of her pensione for a meal. I had to bring her cheese and rolls and eat with her on the bed while my husband toured the streets of Rome, alone.

Ginzburg hated what I wrote. I never could find out why; so my failure was a mystery, a source only of baffled self-loathing. She claimed never to have said what she said, although I had it on tape. I published a thin, incomplete article. We had no more communication.

But at least I had learned something: the great world of European intellectuals and artists, whose imprimatur I dreamed of as my final burnishing, the last, most trustworthy proof of my worth, would not be opened to me. It might no longer exist, or be on the verge of nonexisting, and I imagined a time when I might think of it without a sense of having missed out, or having been kept out. One day, perhaps, I would think of it as a vanished world, like the worlds of the holy pictures and Henry James and Mastroianni: one more world whose pressures and anxieties no longer had their force.

There is no one now, in Rome, whom I visit. I was too embarrassed by my experience of Ginzburg, I felt too much of a failure, to keep up a correspondence with the friend of my English friend. I don't know the real Rome, the Rome of the poor. I don't know anything about it well enough. I know that everything works badly and by corruption. It doesn't matter. I'm not a person who makes money there, who lives by the mind or the moral faculty. When I am there I am a person who lives by the eye.

Each time I come I vow to do more so that I'll be more ready next time. I say I will read more, particularly about the nineteenth-century Romantic travelers in Rome. I will read about the *Risorgimento*. I will learn how to look at the Baroque. I will study more Italian. I will do it regularly, every day. I will buy an Italian grammar book.

But I never do. Is it that I like myself inexpert? The sense of chance? I think I must want to know Rome only a little, as a stranger, a dumb cluck of a tourist, a naive and star-struck lover. One of the girls in *Three Coins in the Fountain*. The youngest, the silliest.

∞∞∞∞∞∞∞∞∞∞∞∞

It is October and I am back in Rome, by myself, here for a few days to wander and to write, on my way to a friend's house in Tuscany. I am, in some ways, a regular, or at least a returning visitor. I know my way to a workman's cafe that makes the perfect pasta *arrabbiata*. The place is without ornament, the dishes prepared simply. I am in love with the waitress with the large nose and the single braid. I think I have had too much wine because after my meal, walking into the square, the sight of a yellow wall covered with ivy and late roses makes me burst into tears. I take myself to a place I have found, another place for quiet in this city of display, a cloister belonging to the confraternity of Saint John. Whoever they are. I have learned, though, that to gain admittance, you don't ring the bell for the cloister, or the confraternity, but another one that says SPOSINI. I learned this from a workman fixing the road after I made three unsuccessful attempts at entrance.

I sit by myself, looking at the spiky rose trees, the last remnants of the summer's wisteria. Over the walls, I can hear cars and music and chatter, but for a moment this place is mine. I am alone and hidden. The stucco walls are light blue. The caretaker wants me gone.

But I don't leave, not for a while, and he disappears into his office. After half an hour, I give him 5,000 lire and I walk the twisted streets of Trastevere, past artisans repairing furniture or making wooden boxes. I make my way back to my hotel near the Campo dei Fiori. I am beginning to get sick. My throat hurts and I am having trouble breathing. Sick in Rome. It seems all wrong and I have heard that Italian doctors go through their entire medical training never looking at a cadaver. So how can I trust them?

That evening I stay in my bed and eat only oranges. I'd planned to go to the catacombs the next morning to get real images of the martyrs who so obsessed my early life. But in the morning, it is raining. I have my breakfast at 7:30, but I decide it's all simply too hard. Despair at the idea of navigating multiple buses in the Roman rain, then standing on line at the catacombs under my inadequate umbrella, bought off the street here from a Somali man, defeats me. I close the shutters and I go back to sleep, falling into one of those filthy sleeps where dreams are perverse and murderous and you wake cleansed and healed.

It is eleven o'clock and the sun is shining. I am well. I will not go to the catacombs. I decide to walk to the Villa Borghese.

How has this happened? I am no longer sick, it is October, warm, the light is golden on the turning leaves, it warms the white stone of the palazzo. The sky, torrentially gray-black three hours ago, is cobalt blue. The pure blue light casts shadows behind the statue of a Roman matron. I sit in the beautiful park, empty and formal. Even the trees look as if they have happily conformed to a design; the cypresses, like folded umbrellas, the skinny pines with their tufted tops, like ladies waving ostrich fans. I have my roll, my cheese, my tomato, bought this morning in the Campo dei Fiori, near the statue of Giordano Bruno, burned by the church as a freethinker. Another kind of martyr, standing eternally in the midst of the fruit sellers, the flower sellers. The air is chilly. I am glad to be wearing the green coat I bought (thinking of Mastroianni) on the Via Veneto, light green, a wool perfect for early (but not deep) winter.

How has this happened to *me?* I am sitting in the golden light in the park among lovers, dogs, and babies. The birds sing, the fountains splash. There is no place I need to be. No one expects me. Nothing is required. How has it happened to me in Rome, that this is who I am, not kneeling to a man in a black robe, or a red robe, or even a white one? On my own, with enough money for a good lunch and a green coat purchased on the Via Veneto. How has it happened to me? How has it come about that I have, to this point, escaped my fate, that I am here, in the sun, under the blue sky, not a martyr? How has it happened that I have become someone who, as a child, I would never even have thought of? Someone I would not have seen on holy cards or in movies. Someone I might not even have read about.

THE
ROOM IN
THE WORLD

THE HOUSE IS IN Truro on Cape Cod; it is the only house that I have ever really loved, the only one that I have yearned to own. I have given it up now, and the pain of these words contains within itself a kernel of pride, like the pride of ending a perfect love affair before its time. But not an unmixed pride because I know I have done it at least partly out of fear. I have been prudent rather than courageous, provident instead of bold.

It is a three-quarters cape at the top of a hilly drive. It is surrounded by a lawn on three sides; one side of the lawn dips abruptly downward and at the bottom of the dip there is a small green where my son and his friends played baseball or threw a tennis ball for our dog. At that top of this hill were placed, habitually, two very light aluminum chaise longues, where I would sometimes sit and watch the children and the dog. At the back of the house is a clothesline where we hung bathing suits and laundry. If we left the laundry until eveningtime, we were set upon by mosquitoes and the air rung with our curses and our vows to vacation anywhere else on earth. There is a gate separating the backyard from the front lawn: white, wooden, ornamental, with curlicues and shapes like a fantasy of acanthus leaves.

When you enter the house you are greeted by steep stairs that lead to an attic door that was closed off to us. The living room has eight windows into which, each of the eight summers that I lived there, the light poured. When I walked into the house for the first time each summer, I felt I hadn't thought about light properly for eleven months, or since the day I'd left.

The woman who once owned the house, who died before I lived there, is someone whose life I very much admire. I met her once or twice at parties and she was kind about my work. She was a writer herself and she supported herself by her pen. She had had three children by three different husbands, and she lived cheaply, imaginatively, spending some years or parts of years in Mexico and the Virgin Islands. She had bought the house from John Dos Passos in the late forties, and it was, as well as her shelter, an occasional source of income when she would rent it, usually to friends.

In beautiful and inexpensive ways, she added richness to the house's New England austerity. She painted the walls of the kitchen to look like Tuscan stucco; they reminded me of the cloister of Santa Croce. The floor of the bedroom was the color of the sea. So in mornings I could walk from the turquoise floor that was the first thing my feet touched, into the kitchen with its rosy walls. The room was dominated by an iron stove that once heated the house, and by a shallow stone sink.

The kitchen was most precious to me in the early mornings when I had it to myself. So many meals I prepared there, resentfully frying eggs for late-rising guests, joyously and anxiously accomplishing a dinner party, neutrally making tuna salad or grilled cheese for family lunches. But it was the mornings I loved best, when I waited for my coffee to bubble up and for my bread to turn itself to toast, and then when I carried them outside onto the low back step. Sometimes I would bring the kitchen mat outside to sit on if the early morning dampness had made the wooden step too wet. I was up at five-thirty. Each morning I did the same thing. I sat on the back step and watched the sky take on its morning color and give up the ghostly imprint of late dawn. I drank my coffee and read ten pages of Proust. The dog would come and sit beside me and I would give her a small piece of my toast.

After my toast and coffee and my Proust, I went upstairs to work. The attic, which had been the owner's bedroom, was the room I claimed for my study. I climbed up steep steps and every time I did I noticed the thick steel handles that the owner had had installed for her support. Even infirm, she did not give up her attic room. The room where she both worked and slept. Sometimes, although I didn't need to, I held on to the steel handles as a tribute to her valour.

In the bathroom upstairs there was a half-empty bottle of bath salts she had used before her death. The books were hers, and I had agreed not to touch them, although I didn't understand why her sons were so insistent upon this point: most of them were paperbacks, and not unusual. But I obeyed in case it was what she wished. I believed that, in death, she liked my being there, that she looked down on me, content.

The floor was covered by straw matting that was pleasantly rough to my bare feet. The desk was long and white, there was a table next to it where I laid out my books. One of the happiest hours of my year was the one just after I arrived, when I unpacked the cartons of books I'd brought (always too many: no one could have read what I brought, everything I dreamed of reading, plus all the books and writers I wanted near me for good luck). I would separate the books, excited by my own discriminations, like a child playing library. The purity of my categorization made me feel blessed. Full of belief in myself, I would sit down for the first time each summer, open my notebook, and set to work.

There is a special attachment to a place in which you have written happily and well. There is nothing to remember about the actual experience of writing well, because you really are not there. The joy of it comes from the removal from life, the sense of having been hurled outside the rim of the world. It is only when you come back from this kind of writing that you are grateful to the place that has gone on being the same while you were out of it; the desk, the chair, the floor, have not rearranged themselves while you were rearranging the universe in words. They waited, faithful brides, for your return. They bathed you with the cool waters and plenishing oint-

ments of their presence and their sameness. Their fidelity
has earned them your eternal love.

And on the bad days, the days when the writing is impossible, you are grateful to them for providing you the
mixed surety and distraction of their physicality. Thank
you, thank you, I would say to the straw matting, to the
white-painted surface of the desk, to the bed with its
black-and-white African print cover which allowed me
to escape from failure into sleep. And above all, I was
grateful to the window for providing me the view over
the tops of trees, the old locusts with their mobile leaves
that were responsive to the wind even when words were
obdurate, that always gave me something to look at: a perfect view for writing, lovely, but not great, suggesting
continuity rather than grandeur. I would never want a
view of a mountain whose intractability would only
replicate the shape of my own mind; a view of water
would be either too beguiling or would convince me of
the futility of my task: for nothing I could make of words
could ever be so satisfying or so various as the movement
of sun on water.

After I had done my four hours of work, it was only
ten o'clock and if I was lucky, everyone in the house
would still be sleeping. I would put into a cloth bag my
pen and notebook, a book of poetry and the nineteenth-
century novel I'd assigned myself that summer (*The Spoils
of Poynton, The Mayor of Casterbridge, Shirley, Romola, The*

Last Chronicle of Barset) and walk through the woods to the bay.

I would shut the front screen door, which provided first the satisfying rasp and squeak of its ancient spring, and then the gentle flap of its closing. I would whistle for the dog. We would make our way first over a small rise where the sun falling hard on the hog cranberry released an excitingly bitter smell. The dog ran away from me, and her high tail swishing through the low leaves of the bushes was a sign of young, animal hope. We walked through a thicket of brush and branches where the light came through only where the branches made a gap. It fell in clots, dollar-size coins on the gray-green or green-yellow of the leaves or the red of the juniper berries, or the white-violet-pink of flowers called bouncing bet or soapwort, which really did smell, when you pressed them, like soap. A few yards uphill through the thicket and then suddenly a clearing and a few feet from that the first glimpse, always a surprise, of water. The bay, silvery or greenish or dark blue, depending on the clouds, and the marsh grasses, feathery or still depending on the wind, and the leaves which I was never around long enough to see turning, only when the wind was high, when they would turn to me their silver undersides.

Always I would stand at the top of the hill overcome with gratitude for the daily surprise of this view of water, dunes, grass, and sea, a beauty which can frighten because you can imagine stepping through a scrim quite easily to a place where there would be nothing but the contemplation of this beauty, a place of silence where the grammar is made up of light, not words, and the only loyalty is to the sun and the horizon.

I never felt that I had looked enough, but I often felt torn between looking and describing in my notebook what I had seen. I made myself move from the high vantage point to my sitting place where, if I was so inclined, I could write something down. I often chose to do that, because after a while the pure looking was too difficult, too powerful: I could never measure up to the demands of looking and for once there was something more difficult than writing, something that made writing seem a way out, a relief.

The only times I didn't feel a need to write as a palliative against the fearful demands of looking were when my son joined me at the bay. We would look together and we would talk about what we were looking at. A rock at low tide, peering through the grayish water. A gull or a duck siting so still we thought they might be stone. Sometimes we came, just the two of us, at sunset and we would name for each other the colors in the changing sky. But for much of the time we would sit silent. With him beside me, I was never afraid that I would lose myself in what I saw.

But most of the time I was alone. It was very quiet when I sat on what I called my couch, a dune made firm by grasses against which I could lean my back. Occasionally, and very far away, though it was only three hundred yards down a gentle slope, people would walk singly or in pairs along the shore. My dog would stand at the top of the dune and bark, outraged by the invasion. I would quiet her, although I was proud of her severity, and it made me feel safe from surprise visitors coming from the woods. I read; I wrote: descriptions or ruminations only, nothing narrative, nothing I could use in something larger, publishable. Sometimes if it was hot, I took off my shirt and let the sand gently abrade my back, enjoying the breeze on my naked breasts. When I was ready to begin reading again I would always put my shirt back on.

I would walk back to the house to find the others now awake, eating, reading the paper, playing cards, and I knew my workday was over. The house, the day, were no longer mine. When I think of the loss of the house, it is not the image of loved ones around the table that seems irreplaceable. Those dear faces can compose themselves into a happy picture in many other pleasant spots. What is irreplaceable is the time in the house when only it and I were awake, when I was dreaming, reading, writing, when its walls were the borders between silence and what is popularly known as real life.

The youngest son of the woman who owned the house owns a small house on the corner of the property, down the hill from the big house and invisible from it. He built the house himself; it is what he does professionally. I found the house because he is a friend of a close friend of mine. The two of them grew up together, winterbound on the Cape.

Of the "washashores," the non–Cape natives, I inhabit a marginal, almost but not quite secure place. In order to have a really secure place, you must have roots that go back to the time when only poor artists and writers and intellectuals came here: before 1940. I got the place I have on account of being considered a serious writer, and because I came originally because of a connection to the old bohemians. I was brought here first by a woman who had summered in the house since 1933 and some years lived there year-round. She was one of those artistic and experimental people who lived on nothing in the Wellfleet woods. You could live cheaply in the Cape then; it was one of the places, like the Village, where you could live cheaply, where now you need a lot of money to live. My friend who is an artist can have a house here because her father, a writer, bought one in the twenties, and left it to her after his death. My other friends who have houses, as my mother would have said, "come from money." There is no one of my generation to whom I am close who bought a house only on the money that she or he earned.

When she talked about wealthy people, my mother would say: "She comes from money." I would imagine babies coming into the world not bloody from their mother's womb, but bursting through, then sliding down, a hill of gold coins. My mother spoke of such people in a tone which marked her mixed awe and contempt for those who didn't work as hard as she did. She never allowed herself to be close to such people, or perhaps she never had the opportunity to, but I have. And usually it doesn't make any difference, because I have never before much wanted anything that they could have that I could not. Until now, until this summer when the youngest son of the woman who owned the house told me that it was possible the house would be for sale.

I had always believed, on no evidence at all, that the house would be mine. That when it was put up for sale something would happen. A movie sale. A MacArthur. A miracle. A windfall legacy, or Michael Anthony, personal secretary to Beresford Tipton, the TV millionaire. I would take my place beside my friends, the heirs of the old bohemians; I would carry on the line of writers and artists who had, for years, looked at those views, written or painted in that light, wept and laughed and eaten and drunk in those houses with their transcendentalist beams.

I was given what is called the right of first refusal because the youngest son, who had been our landlord for eight years, knew we were interested and, loving his mother, wanted someone whom she would have found congenial to have the house. He told us the price. It was a fair price, by the standards of the market, but I could not possibly afford it. When I first read the numbers on the page, I fell into immediate despair. Then I began speculating wildly. I could sell everything I had. I could sign up a pop book and get a big advance and use it for a down payment. I could use the money I had saved for my daughter's education, which wasn't required now because, in choosing the university at which I taught, her tuition was exempt. I had said I would save that money for graduate school, medical school, law school but I thought: I will spend it on the house, and when I die it will be hers.

After a weekend of head-spinning financial speculation, when I thought the house was mine, I called my accountant. He didn't even turn on his computer to look up my files. "It's impossible," he said. "People who earn what you earn don't have houses that cost that much. It would be a disaster for you."

A disaster. That was impossible. I knew what disasters were: tornadoes, famines, plagues. It would be nothing of the sort.

I kept reiterating my plans.

"Look," he said. "Is that what you want? Having to write things you don't want to write because of a house? Not being able to turn in a book late if you want to spend more time on it because you need to meet a mortgage payment? Do you really want to live like that?"

No, I didn't really want to live like that. Part of what the house would give me, what I loved it for, was a sense of peace. And I could not have peace if I woke every morning worried about money, facing a book or article I had no appetite for, the prospect of which filled me with dread. And I was frightened of all sorts of other things that could happen to a house. I was frightened of dry rot and burst pipes and guests who forgot to put the shower curtain in and soaked the floor straight through and oil tanks that leaked poisonously into the grass and the water supply, of septic tanks that overflowed and cracks in chimneys, and walls that turned the consistency of wet paper, walls that could crumble if you put a pencil point into them, although why I focused on putting a pencil point into a wall I did not know. I was too afraid of things: of ruin or anxiety about ruin, to take the risk that owning the house required.

I told the youngest son I couldn't take the house.

So I have given the house up because of money. This has made me learn something about myself and money that I might have preferred not to know. I have never before really wanted anything that money could buy. Or no, that isn't really true. What I mean is that I have never really wanted anything I couldn't afford to buy. I own one thing that is worth a lot of money, a pastel by a great artist. I am afraid to say his name here on account of the possibility of theft. Just forming that sentence makes me frightened about the power of money, its power to arouse desire and hatred, to induce secrecy and fear.

I was brought up believing not one good thing about money. Burned into my soul were the words of Jesus: "You cannot serve God and mammon." "Find for yourself treasure in heaven." "Consider the lilies of the field." Of the deadly sins, I prided myself on being free of avarice. Even its syllables seemed alien to me, nothing I could hold easily in my mouth. They were an irritant, those sounds, like a canker sore, unlike those other sin-bearing syllables, swamps in which I could so easily and terribly drown: sloth, lust. Or that staircase, gluttony, down which I could plummet to my doom. Or those shining swords on which my soul could be impaled: pride, anger, envy. Now I understand the taste of avarice, bitter as aloes, cold and tart. I understand because the taste is on my tongue.

And what losing the house says about my life fills my lungs with a rich oxygen made up of self-pity and self-contempt. What am I fit for, I ask myself, and answer, Well, not much. The woman who owned the house would, I believe, have taken risks to keep it. She would have done her journalistic scut work with equanimity, knowing it was for the house. I wonder what it would have meant if, in one of her lean years, she had needed a new roof.

But I have come to the conclusion that what she would have felt if her beautiful house had needed a new roof is so different from what I would have felt that there is no sense even comparing the responses. At the sound of a strong wind, my heart would have been in my mouth. When I sat down to write, I would have been computing sums in the margins of my notebook: estimates by the roofer, what I could make on journalism. What I would lose to taxes.

The woman who owned the house did not write much. She died an old woman and, thirty years younger than she was when she died, I have already written more.

What does that mean? It does not, of course, necessarily mean that what I have written is better. It does mean, probably, that I recognize myself most clearly by what I've written. Or I have up to this time. She recognized or knew herself, importantly, as a person who owned that house and land. I am afraid that, in having to know myself that way, I would know myself less by what I've written.

I dislike myself for being unwilling to take the risk, as I dislike myself for envying people whose fathers left them money or property or trust funds, or women who married men who entered high-paying professions, or other writers who have houses on expensive tracts of land.

And I dislike myself for being unwilling to devote myself to something beautiful, to sacrifice time and equanimity for something my eyes would fall upon, every day, with joy. I think of people who can never marry, who only go from lover to lover, because they cannot say in sickness or in health. I have a new sympathy for them. I am one of them.

But everything the house stands for—clarity, simplicity, solidity—is betrayed by these kinds of thoughts. I suppose that bereft lovers are prey to unworthy thoughts. And I am, in relation to this house, bereft. Some mornings, I am simply full of gratitude for the house and what it gave me for the time it could. But other mornings I wake up, half sick with longing and heavy with the weight of what I cannot have.

I will not go back there again. But it was never likely that, coming from where I came from, I would have got to go there at all, to say nothing of having spent eight summers there. As a child, I would have thought a week in a Cape

Cod motel was something only to be dreamed of. Now I feel I have lost my birthright. Something that should be given to me as a result of my original life, my devotion to literature. I carried on about this to my friends until they all grew tired of it. One said to me, "It's not *The Cherry Orchard;* it's not like the place has been in your family for generations and you can hear the sound of the ax going *chop-chop-chop.*"

So I must put all this in perspective. I cannot afford to buy something that I wanted, something outside the reach of 99.5 percent of the human race. This is not tragedy, only at best tragicomic. I have lost something I never had. I have given back what I only borrowed.

And whatever made me think that devotion to literature was rewarded by beautiful houses? This was the sort of thing I never thought about; when I thought of writing, I thought I would be poor, and that, perhaps if I were lucky, I'd be published. How outsize are our appetites, how easily jaded. How quickly we grow gluttonous, our eyes half closed, our necks thick with excess. How easily what would once have seemed an unattainable luxury begins to seem a necessity, its absence a deprivation, a proof of the injustice of the world.

I will not go back there. I will not sit on the back step and see the sky take on its color, or walk over the hill for the first glimpse of gray-blue water, or watch from my desk the locust leaves turn over in the wind. My time in the house was a gift, a gift that wasn't meant to last. I should never have called it mine. But the house, in its embrace of me, seduced me. Like many an overeager lover, I misheard its whispers. I got the breathy "I am yours . . . ," but missed the final syllables, provisional and hesitating: ". . . only for a while."

BOULEVARDS OF
THE IMAGINATION

FROM THE PLACE where I stand at the top of this hill there is a view, a glimpse, rather, of river. In some seasons, like this one, late summer, it is far more glimpse than view. There is a thick curtain of trees and then, cut out, a hand-size triangle of pewter or of tin.

This hill is not really a hill but a narrow street beginning at the gates of a university campus. Columbia: designed by the murdered Stanford White, shot by a madman for a woman's love. Even the blueprints of the place are soaked in narrative.

The first time I stood at the top of this hill was in the spring of 1966. My two friends and I had just been admitted to Barnard and we were coming to look in on some classes on a day off from our Catholic school in Queens. It must have been a Holy Day of Obligation, otherwise there would have been no reason for Barnard to be in session while we were free. Perhaps it was Holy Thursday or the Feast of the Ascension. Perhaps we lied to our parents and said we would go to Mass first.

Was it a punishment for that lie that led us to get off the subway at the wrong One Hundred Sixteenth Street—One Hundred Sixteenth and Lenox Avenue? The man in the token booth took one look at our clothes and faces and guessed our mistake without our having to say anything. "This isn't Broadway, girls," he said, as if we were hick starlets with straw valises. He told us to take the subway back down to Forty-second Street, then the shuttle, then the West Side train uptown. We didn't listen. We walked across One Hundred Sixteenth Street, through Harlem, through Morningside Park, fearless, pretending we felt at home, knowing that our parents would be appalled.

I remember seeing the green roofs of Columbia and feeling a sense of rightness that stayed with me as I crossed the street to Barnard's Millbank Hall, where I climbed the marble staircase to the admissions office. From there I was sent to Barnard Hall, where the English classes were. I got off the elevator and looked in the mirror on the fourth floor of Barnard Hall. I said to myself, Yes, I'm here.

Thirty-two years later (almost the entire life span of Jesus Christ) I stand in front of the same mirror, a teacher now, waiting for the same elevator. And again I say to myself, Yes (but perhaps with more emphasis on the monosyllable), yes, I'm here.

But what do I mean by here? And how did I get here? Or more properly, how did I get back?

*   *   *

On my first journeys to "here" (I called it "the city" then) I was, of course, accompanied. My first journeys were, naturally, with my parents. I would like to say with my father, but that was not always or entirely the case. Sometimes I traveled with both parents. A journey divided into parts. The first by car, a drive from our town (now I must say it), a suburb of New York, the first town over the city line, but nevertheless we didn't pay, as my mother was glad to point out, "those city taxes." How early did I feel misplaced there, or is it only looking back, and only in comparison, that the sense of misplacement grew up? I was conscious, being dressed in my stiff clothes, my hat tied under my chin with chafing ribbons or secured by an abrading elastic band, of traveling to somewhere more important than the place we lived, or the place we gave as our address. Probably it was my mother who drove us in our black Oldsmobile from Valley Stream to the parking lot near the One Hundred Sixty-ninth Street subway stop in Jamaica; probably my mother because she believed herself, with some justification, a better driver than my father. Anyway, she owned the car.

It was on these trips, especially the ones with my father, that I learned to love great public buildings. They came into my life naturally in that we didn't visit them especially, we were on our way to someplace else, to see someone else, and the buildings just happened to be there.

My first large public buildings were the great New York churches where we would stop to "make a visit," that is, to engage in private prayer, or perhaps to catch a

noontime or five o'clock Mass. We would go to Saint
Patrick's if we were on the way to Radio City, to Saint
Jean Baptiste on Lexington if we were visiting my father's
old friend from his Cleveland days, who also lived on
Lexington, a street name that I liked because it had a
nickname: Lex. Or to Saint Francis Xavier on Sixteenth
Street, because my father had a friend who lived as door-
keeper to the Jesuit community there.

Although these churches were sacred spaces whose
function was arguably the same as any parish church, the
spaciousness, the ornamentation, the obvious expense
involved in their creation and maintenance, made these
churches seem irreligious to me. I may have pretended to
pray there, may in fact have gone through the motions of
praying, but I was really not praying, but looking.

I was gathering information.

In these great buildings I felt I had traveled abroad.
Clearly, they had more to do with Europe than with
America. I sensed quite early on that all important things
happened in Europe. We were as a nation informal,
makeshift, and spontaneous. Greatness, I believed, must
have to do with embellishment and formality, painstak-
ingly hard won. From these churches' architectural
details, I was learning crucial things about life overseas.
The lanterns under the arches, the ornamental capitals,
the lunettes free of devotional figures, with patterns,
instead, of natural objects (wings, flowers, leaves), the
quality of expansive darkness, the shadings of gray light,
the sound of heels on the stone floors reverberating

upward to the vaulted ceilings, the temperature of the holy water in the marble fonts, the ironwork letters POORBOX on the top of the box with the slit for coins: I would take in all of these with the same sense of urgency with which I took in the colored illustrations of my English picture books. Books my father brought home from the city. For me and for me only. No one else I knew had books whose illustrations specialized in the deep, refined, reserved, mysterious colors: ochres, teals, burnt siennas, *ombres roses.*

In the same way that I don't remember praying in any of the churches, I don't remember looking at any pictures in the Metropolitan Museum or reading any books in the New York Public Library. It was being there that was important, walking up and down the Met's great staircase, looking at the white-and-gold ceilings of the public library. Passing through, visiting somewhere that was part of the life my father lived without my mother, a life I knew had something to do with writing, since when people asked what his job was, I would say "a writer."

In my memory, my father and I were always silent in these buildings. It may have been because we knew they didn't have to do with our individual biographies, our personal fates, the series of events we had lived through before we got there, the accidents that had befallen us and made us only who we were. Impossible to think of saying "I" in these great halls; to express preference or dismay, affection or discomfort, to bring up the past or our familial ties. Or was it simply that my father was too absorbed to talk to me? It was a rich, loamy silence that we breathed, made possible only by the volume of dim or light air.

And then we were outside and on the sidewalk. I was my father's girl again, only a child; I had to hold his hand. Only together would we pass as real New Yorkers.

On the streets I knew that we would soon be in other kinds of rooms, closed in and darker than the ones we lived in, rooms in the apartments of my father's friends. It was on our way to one of these that my father and I would walk up Central Park West. I was particularly fond of Central Park West because it was a way that my real appetites, which were urban, could include nature.

I knew from my reading that I was supposed to long for nature. I didn't, though, not even the great forests in fairy tales, the crashing turquoise seas, the vast and snowy mountains. As an idea they tired me, but I could look at the trees of Central Park West, allow my eye to travel quickly to a glass canopy. I would not be entrapped in nature, where there were no stories I could tell to point out my distinction. Nature was there on Central Park West to be talked about; even the bald outcropping of sheer rock was there only for an effect. It was possible to walk on the side of Central Park West where there was a wall separating the street from the park, and to forget about the park, casting your eyes only on the buildings. The playing children, the lovers reclining on the grass, the water, the birds, the rows of trees, all these were separated by the stone wall which seemed to communicate only with the elegant buildings, not with the unbridled life it kept from view. I had only to

cross the street and speak to a doorman, who would place
his white-gloved hand on the brass doorknob and show
me into the lobby with a crystal chandelier, to redress the
right balance of my understanding of the world. A moment
from that outcropping of rock, I could be on my way in an
elevator to poetry and music. All that was waiting for me if
I could simply find the right building, only say aloud the
correct syllables of the names whose sounds would provide
me with everything important I needed for the proper
presentation of my real self.

It seemed wonderful to me that these buildings had
names: the San Remo, the Prasada, the El Dorado, the
Kennilworth. Names with no meaning for me except that
they were foreign. I was interested only in the foreign
sound, I had no concern for what the names might mean.
Now I can speculate on the varieties of transatlantic
dreams—Venetian, Scottish, Castilian, English Renaissance. But, then, if I had tried to make pictures of the
originals, what would I have seen? A gondola, men in
kilts, a woman snapping castanets, a courtier with a ruff. I
wouldn't have understood the implications of this hungry
impulse to appropriate. Why would I? I wasn't interested
in implications. Only in the foreign sounds, suggesting
the important continent, the Europe of the war that had
ended just four years before my birth. Four years, but
another era, barely recognizable. The pastness of the past is
not always evenly spread.

What is the source of my images of the war? I will not
say the Holocaust, because that is a word I learned only
later, much later; it is not a word that pressed itself on the

soft wax of my childhood. So where did these images
originate, so strong, so frightening, so precious to me? I
was proud of knowing about them as if even the knowing
made me European. But I don't know how I got the
knowledge. We did not have television. I don't remember
seeing the images on movie screens. The images were not
of piled-up corpses. They were images of hiding people,
hidden people, hunted people. Families, particularly children. I heard the word *refugee,* and although I was frightened by it, I imagined people of great distinction,
musicians in particular, wandering through dark forests,
starving. Then a blank. Then they are on a ship, in their
stiff, foreign coats, their round-toed, heavy shoes, their
rimless glasses. Then they are met coming off the ship and
taken in a taxi right to Central Park West, to these buildings, to rooms which I imagine to be quite dark although
there are large windows that give out onto the park,
allowing in my mind for a view but no illumination.
There, served by maids who are also refugees, they play
their violins and read their poetry and their philosophy
and understand that never, never again will they be made
to suffer.

I never met any people like the people I thought of,
nor did I ever enter a room like the ones I imagined. But
I did, several times, go into an apartment on Central Park
West, and that must be why I walked there so often with
my father.

We were there on business. We were there, not listening to people play their violins or read their poetry, or
looking at their views, but because my father wanted a

man he'd known before he came from New York to invest in one of his magazines. Known from the Midwest, from Ohio, where my father was still a Jew. I don't know whether he brought me to put pressure on the potential donor or simply for the treat of being with me. With my father, either is possible. I didn't understand what we were doing there; I can't imagine what I might have guessed. We walked into a dark living room with drawn, gravy-colored drapes. We were greeted by a man with a bald head, rimless glasses, a cigar, rolls of fat above his collar that alarmed me for his health. I don't know if the rolls of fat bothered me before or after the time he told my father, "I've got a boil on the back of my neck. I have to soak it." And, right there in the living room, he, astonishingly, archaically, atavistically, removed the collar from his shirt. He showed my father a large, reddish swelling. So that was a boil. What did it have to do with boiling? Was it a source of heat, was there a liquid inside it, bubbling and roiling? He had said he was going to soak the boil, but on the table, there was only a small blue bowl with a white towel beside it. Was he going to lie on the table so that his neck fell into the bowl? I was taken by the maid into the kitchen, so I never knew.

Silently, and with no interest in me, she put on the counter, in front of which I sat on a high wooden stool, a plate of butter cookies and a glass of milk. I didn't like milk. I always imagined the warm body of the cow it came from and I was disgusted. But I was afraid to refuse anything offered to me in these high rooms, with their husbanded light, and their decorative surfaces that absorbed sound so that what was apprehensible was the pure atmosphere of prosperity, which I had not the slightest inclination to resist. I felt too grateful that I had been allowed inside one of the apartments in one of the buildings with a name.

It must have been after the expeditions with my father that we went to the Museum of Natural History. I always felt uncomfortable there at first, an imposter, an intruder, afraid I would not know what I should be looking at or looking for, and what to say, or even what could be said about what I'd seen. In the rotunda, I had to think of Teddy Roosevelt. There was a showcase for his hats: a police helmet, a top hat, a pith helmet covered by netting delicate as a veil. Teddy Roosevelt frightened me. I was afraid of his teeth, square cut. They seemed made for grinding, grinding up little girls like me who would not measure up to the ideals of the outdoor life. I was made to feel unworthy by his words cut into the stone walls of the rotunda: *daring, courage, iron endurance, self-mastery.*

In the rotunda, I felt in danger. But leaving the rotunda, danger was transformed. Once I could forget the shaming words cut into the walls, I could feel assured. Danger would be kept far from us, by men like Teddy Roosevelt, rich, athletic, Protestant. Danger became dimness, a dimness I very much liked. And I liked the sense of walking through a dream, even though I knew it wasn't my dream, but a usurpation of someone else's. I knew this was a boy's dream, or a dream made up for boys.

I loved losing myself in the dioramas, their painted backgrounds, floral or leafy, endlessly distant, endlessly reassuring. I could allow myself to become lost in images, the atmosphere of dawn or twilight, the stasis of the mammals, their gestures stopped at a certain inevitable moment, pointing to a vista. Behind this glass nothing could die, or perhaps death had already happened, and so was benign. In this atmosphere, nothing was required of me. There was nothing I needed to say. I only had to stop from time to time and point at what I saw, and then move on, past the dinosaurs, whose huge angularity I wanted to get by quickly, to the room of ocean life, the huge blue whale, the half-naked black figure diving for pearls, the manatee immersed in unclear water, the polar bear and harp seal, the one vision of shed blood a patch of red on snow. Except for that one sight of red, the colors were mercifully subdued. Uncertainty was a blessing there; clarity was not all; I moved from dimness to darkness, until finally I made my way to the planetarium, where I leaned my head back in the total darkness and heard a deep voice talk about the stars where I believed the dead were, and were happy.

Then I could walk into the light again, holding my father's hand, and enter, once again, the world of language, full of movement and a promise that included people like myself. "San Remo, Prasada, El Dorado, Kennilworth," I would say, full of belief in what these names contained and would, one day, unlock.

After my father's death, there were years I did not travel to the city much, and I only walked on Central

Park West in my imagination. And while I was reading a particular book, the *Reader's Digest* condensed books edition of *Marjorie Morningstar,* which belonged to my aunt who lived with my grandmother. My grandmother's house had very few books in it, and most of them were pious. The set of *Reader's Digest* condensed books was in the house because my aunt had brought them home from work; the plant at which she worked as a keypunch operator was somehow connected to the distribution of *Reader's Digest* condensed books.

I radically envied Marjorie her good fortune, envied everything from the elevator with a bench where you could sit during your ride, to the poor protective uncle, to the prosperous father with his endless admiration for his beautiful daughter and his endless willingness to pay for her clothes. A beautiful girl, a cherished girl, a protected girl. Desired, but never in danger. Each morning from her window she saw the trees of the park, the skyline of Manhattan. I placed myself in her beautifully crafted shoes, I walked the borders of her temporary misery where I could move away from the rules and wishes of my family, but always return safe. To the power of the elevator, and a father in a satin dressing gown, and the view, hers for the looking anytime she wanted, of lights that glittered far superior to any constellation, any frigid planet, any far and approachless heaven where a lovely girl might be forever swallowed up.

*   *   *

Later, I went into one of the buildings where Marjorie
Morningstar might have lived when I had no business,
really no business being there. I was no longer the solitary
little girl, holding on to her father's hand. I had become
an adventurer; I had friends; I had been on dates. My girlfriends had known for a couple of years what I had always
known: that real life was lived in the city, the life we
wanted but were not born to. Although it is possible that
I, with my glamorous dead father, may have been born to
it, and they, daughters of workingmen, simpler and less
valuable for being still alive, looked to me for permission
to enter a world I had already visited but had been forced
to leave, the exiled daughter of the defunct king. Lying to
our parents, we took the bus from Long Island or
Queens, to the subway, the F train in Jamaica, where we
sometimes got out at Lexington Avenue and Fifty-ninth
Street, and sometimes at Columbus Circle. If we got out
at Lexington, we walked to Bloomingdale's, where we
bought something, a Yardley colorless lip gloss maybe, so
that we could have one of the sky blue shopping bags
with the beautiful woman in pigtails who was saying,
"Eyes closed [and hers were] I buy everything at Bloomingdale's." We pretended we were shopping for our
wardrobes (we used the word *wardrobe*), that we had a fortune to spend on clothes, all the clothes we could possibly
want for college, and that they were being delivered to
Our Apartment on Central Park West.

   If we got off at Columbus Circle, we walked up Central Park West pretending we were on our way to the

Majestic or the San Remo. How light we were, girls pretending, but knowing that surely something was in store
for us, richer and more colorful than the houses we snuck
out of, saying we were going to a meeting of the Catholic
Forensic League at a Manhattan Catholic school. Regis.
Marymount.

It was 1965. Skirts were short, haircuts were geomet-
ric, eyeliner was worn thick and Egyptian, the Beatles
were in London, we wore Mary Janes as we had as little
girls, not getting the joke—we were still little girls and
everyone knew it but us. The leaves on the trees were
fragile and lime green, the sun sparkled off the shining
brasses of the doors and cupolas, the spotless gloves of the
doormen were white as snow.

One of my friends was fearless. "Come on," she said.
She walked up to the doorman of the San Remo. "I have
to wait in the lobby for my cousins," she said in a fake
English accent. "What are your cousins' names," the doorman asked. "Smith," she said, giving him a don't-you-dare
look. Probably he knew we were lying, but he let us sit on
the couch in the lobby saying "tally-ho," and "cheerio,"
and "ra*ther.*" Then we ran up the street laughing, holding
each other up, blissfully weakened by laughter. "He
thought we were waiting for our cousins. The Smiths, can
you believe?" Each breath was delicious, stolen as it was
from the air paid for by rich men who were not our
fathers or the fathers of our boyfriends or the fathers of
anyone we knew. We did not say it to each other but we
imagined ourselves walking into these doorways, money
in our purses, our arms full of packages from Blooming-

dale's which we set down on the table in the foyer—we called it a foyer although it is a word we had never used—and saying, "Darling, I'm home," to the distinguished husband who hands us a martini and says, "Come look at the view, darling. All this is mine, and now it's yours."

I believe that everything I have just spoken of—the grand churches, the museums and the libraries, the rocks and trees and buildings, the books and movies, the glimpse of the inside of an apartment, above all the companionship and daring of my friends—all this was required in order that I could get from where I was, the house that had been my grandmother's, to here, a here that in the style of Stephen Dedalus's list would properly be described:

> my apartment
> Barnard College
> Columbia University
> Morningside Heights
> The Upper West Side
> New York City
> The World

It is far more likely that I would be writing this at a cluttered table in a ruinous kitchen in the house my mother had grown up in that she and I had allowed to decay. An unadorned and heavy woman, friendless, unmated, caring for my ailing mother as she took care of hers, leaving in the mornings for my job as a schoolteacher or librarian, returning at night to feed and bathe my mother and to eat and drink myself into a stupor, watching old movies in front of a too-small TV beside my mother's bed. But no, the picture is wrong. Living there, like that, I would not be writing.

I am not there, I am here, in this apartment provided by Barnard College and Columbia University. It is possible to say that I have earned it by writing and devotion to literature: no one has earned it for me, and in this I take a great, perhaps an overweening pride. But that's not right, I haven't earned it; or earning is not the point: it is great good luck that has allowed me to be back where I belong. When we moved here ten years ago, after eighteen years of what I considered rustication, that is to say, life in a small town ninety miles up the Hudson, the same river that I glimpse from the top of the hill, I made the children sing a song with me as we drove up the block. "Claremont Avenue here we come/Right back where Mom started from." I had replaced the name California—that other land of dreams—with the name of our new street.

When I first came here, in 1967, the world that I thought I was traveling to, a world of formality, embellishment, grandeur, and fineness, was in the process of disappearing. Or at least of being so radically questioned in precisely those aspects I had dreamed of that I had no time to revel in my dearly bought reward.

No sooner had I arrived at Barnard, in the clothes I'd saved my summer wages to buy, clothes whose labels I had coveted—Villager, Papagallo, Pendelton—that I realized they were all wrong, and a person wearing those clothes was not the person I wanted to be at all. I had hardly got to know my new friends—non-Catholics from places like Missouri and North Dakota—when I was, along with my two old friends from high school, riding on a bus to Washington to the Pentagon march, for which I bought a new pair of bell-bottomed jeans.

Only now do I understand the speed at which we then were forced to travel. In six months, we went from processions where we crowned a statue of the Virgin with a wreath of flowers to linking hands with strangers, learning what to do in case of tear gas or cops run amok. The same girls who in the spring had been singing, "O Mary we crown thee with blossoms today/Queen of the Angels, Queens of the May," were chanting, the following autumn, "Hey, hey LBJ, how many kids did you kill today?"

And in my second semester of freshman year at Columbia, the riots occurred. A year earlier I had been presiding over student council meetings where we had to decide on an appropriate punishment for girls who'd been caught getting into a car with a boy while still in uniform; now I was sitting in on teach-ins on the lawn in front of Butler Library where we contemplated "burning the whole fucking place down."

I had to hide my horror at the idea of destroying those marble staircases, the reading room with its long, monastic tables and its crystal chandeliers and its beautiful books that smelled of learning. But I had to believe that property was less important than the flesh of children, which was being burned by the napalm that was manufactured by Dow Chemical, from which the university accepted money. I had to understand that the ornate green roofs remained intact, the lights in the chandeliers were kept lit, because of money earned from the burning flesh of children. And I knew that if I had to cast my lot with some group, it had to be the group pledged to stop the burning of children's flesh. I knew this, not from my new friends, or from what I was learning in my classes or in teach-ins, but from the words of the Gospel: "Where your treasure lies, there also doth your heart lie."

I prayed that the beautiful buildings would not be burned down, that the beautiful books would not be destroyed. I prayed furtively, guiltily; I wouldn't have dreamt of going into a church. The archdiocese was presided over by Cardinal Spellman, a great supporter of Vietnam. If I went into a church, everyone would know I was having sex, and would order me to stop, and I knew I wouldn't because I liked it much too much. I understood that there were priests who opposed the war, but they were saying folk masses, and I couldn't stand singing about transubstantiation to the tune of Peter, Paul and Mary songs, and I suspected they loved themselves too much for consecrating whole wheat bread instead of Hosts, and that, despite the antiwar protest and the whole wheat bread, they would still be telling me to stop having sex. I needed formality, but formality was in the hands of men who were shouting about communism and free love, just as the country was in the hands of men who were lying about burning the flesh of children.

It was hard for me to recognize the world. Not only was I not a virgin, I was in love with a homosexual; my friends were dealing drugs and having abortions. Some days we lay around all day in an apartment on One Hundred Nineteenth Street, where not only the walls but the windows were painted black. We listened to Joplin and Hendrix and the Stones; *Marjorie Morningstar* and Bloomingdale's and the Museum of Natural History were never mentioned. We were sometimes surprised when we went outside to find that the sun was still shining.

But I did not stop going to my classes, except during the riots. Except for those weeks, I went on entering the buildings of Barnard, which comforted me with their solidity—their bookish smell, the width of the staircase, the cool stone of the banisters. I was taught by women who told me I was gifted, well-born women with hair hanging down their backs or in coiled blond knots at their napes, who introduced me to Chaucer and Spenser and Auden, elegant men in houndstooth jackets who smoked pipes and told of people whose names I confused: Arthur Henry Hallam, Arthur Hugh Clough.

I discovered that the Romantic poets were not romantic and that I did not like them, except for Keats; that I preferred the Renaissance. So after reading Sidney and Donne and Herbert and Marvell and the Revenge Tragedians, I took a course on Tasso and Ariosto, taught by an Italian, and on Ronsard, taught by a Russian Jew brought up in France. I would hear a snatch of Hindemith or Monteverdi and spend the day in the library listening to music, earphones on my head like a radio announcer. I discovered the paintings of Van Eyck and took the bus across town on Friday afternoons to the Metropolitan to see them, forgetting that, only a short time before, I had prayed to the Madonnas that the other people in the museum only looked at and that because of that I had more in common with the kneeling donors than I did with the people I stood beside.

I could sense the material of my mind thinning, spreading, growing transparent; sometimes I was feverish with the excitement of what I was learning and my eyes felt dry and hot and overlarge, the skin around them felt abraded. After hours studying in the library, I would walk outside and the color of the sky at six o'clock on an October evening—slate blue, shot through with black— seemed as inviting and dangerous as if I were a child playing too late, too hard, and at any minute I might be called in. But I was not called in. I was told to stay out later, to travel farther: the world of ideas was mine. I belonged there; I could inhabit any region of it. My body, both overexcited and repressed from all that reading, would insist on movement. I would run down the hill toward Riverside Drive and let the wind bite into me, hear the buzz of the cars and watch the lights come on across the river.

My friends and I took the subway downtown to see movies starring Holly Woodlawn and we speculated that she might be a real genius and that maybe drag queens were on the existential cutting edge, and we wondered if we had to listen to the thinkers who told us that if we really loved our bodies we would eat our own menstrual blood. I knew myself a poet, but I didn't want to be a fake, like some others I suspected, so I set myself tasks so that I could honor my calling. I wrote villanelles and curtal sonnets and ghazals and translated from the Italian and revised all night. A teacher suggested that I might really be a fiction writer and I said, "No, of course I'm not, I'm a poet": I am (can't you see) in love with form and its restrictions, so different from the unrestricted life which, as a poet, I intended to live.

And, most every night, unless I lied and said I was at a girlfriend's studying (I was probably in someone's bed, someone I may or may not have known well), even after days which I spent occupying buildings, I took the train back to my mother's house. My grandmother's house. Every night when I came home, my mother made us supper in the increasingly ramshackle kitchen, then went to bed where she drank herself into a stuporous sleep. In the room that my high school boyfriend and I painted yellow, where the skeleton of the dead bird might, for all I knew, still have been, I talked on the phone to my friends coming down from bad acid trips or coming home from parties at Warhol's Factory.

But I turned in my papers; and I wrote more poetry than anyone, and Barnard rewarded me. I won all the literary prizes. One summer I was given a grant so that for the first time since I was fifteen I didn't have to work in an office for a whole summer. Instead, I studied Italian, like one of the girls who could go home to Central Park West. That summer I told my mother I was getting a room in the newly built dorm, on One Hundred Twenti-eth Street and Amsterdam, that I would pay for it. The week before I was to move in, she fell and fractured her leg in three places. Heartlessly, I refused to give up my plans for the dorm, and I arranged for one of her cousins to care for her. The cousin made it clear that she thought I was a selfish monster. I paid no attention. I came home every weekend to a house where the dust made me asth-matic and I ate sweet foods to the point of nausea, and past it, to the point of retching in the toilet of the gray bathroom that I had never liked.

After college, I could not stay in the city; I had to get away from my mother's house and she wouldn't stand for me living in New York, in an apartment with my friends, rather than home with her "for free" if I was only work-ing at a job. But she respected education, and to get away from her I went to graduate school in a city in western New York where I found nothing beautiful, and to get away from there I married.

I married the man who told me I didn't deserve to live in a house and I left him for someone who told me there was nothing good enough for me. I moved into his house. We had two children there. I liked the house, but it never seemed mine. I longed to go back home. To the city. To be "here." And I am here now.

*   *   *

It is four-thirty in the morning. I am awakened by the
sound of a marauding band of students shouting and
breaking bottles on the sidewalk. I call 911, but the hooli-
gans disappear before the cops arrive. I decide to get up.
The darkness is precious; what it obscures is mine, chosen, treasured, nothing I need to fear. The wooden floors
creak at my step, but I know which boards creak and how
to avoid them if I need to. In the living room, the con-
tents of my son's backpack are spread out on the floor; on
the coffee table there are too many books and magazines
and newspapers, and on the shelf next to the television
there are too many videotapes and CDs. I have not been
able to break the curse of uneasy habitation. I see the creation of domestic order as time taken away from reading,
writing, talking, being with friends or in the world, and
although I am sometimes choked with regret and shame
at not maintaining a beautiful abode, I do not change my
ways. My daughter's room is empty; she is living across
the street, in one of the green-roofed buildings of
Columbia; she, too, has had my dream of New York as the
great good place; she chose to go to college here. In the
small back room, the maid's room, the tiniest in the apartment (but it has its own sink and toilet, I tell myself, so as
not to feel guilty that I have chosen the largest room in
the apartment for my own study), my son sleeps, his long,
heavy miasmic adolescent sleep. I look at him from the
doorway; I restrain myself from going in to kiss him; he is

fifteen now, and there are certain things I can no longer do and will never be able to do again. His room smells like a man's; no longer does the yeasty smell of a child's sweat pervade the air. He is a man now, and my daughter is in the world. Soon I will be living without children. Soon my study will be the center of the house.

I turn the light on in the kitchen, dark because of the hour and because its windows bring no natural light. I make my coffee, eat my toast, my orange: the breakfast I have every day, a meal which fills me with a ridiculous sense of well-being. These are the hours I like most, when everyone is asleep and the place is mine and I can move from my own dream life to the life of writing. On the walls of my study are pictures of Colette, Emma Goldman, Akhmatova, Katherine Anne Porter, Jean Stafford, Marina Tsvetayeva, and my father. A drawing of our dining room made by my son when he was ten. Snapshots of places I have been happy: a house in Cape Cod, a porch with a wooden table on which is set a bowl of plums. Color xeroxes of paintings of my beloved friend. A photograph of Pope John XXIII, given to me by my friend, a priest whose church I now feel I can go to. The Parish of the Holy Cross across the street from the Port Authority. It is not one of the grand Baroque or Gothic churches that fed my imagination as a child. It's a Victorian pile, although it was Louis Comfort Tiffany's favorite New York church, and there are three of his windows there. I can enter this building comfortably, feeling neither like a stranger nor an intruder, simply a member of the congregation. A congregation which includes the mad, the derelict, the stars of soap operas, and some of the old Irish who've been in this parish since it was Father Duffy's of the Fighting 69th. No one will shout from the pulpit here about communism and free love, or even about abortion or divorce. In this place, I feel free, once again, to pray. This place which is so valuable to me because in New York, which so prides distinction, no one need be distinguished to enter.

The great buildings I staked my dreams on are no longer marked for me by their emptiness. I use them; they are places where I work. I no longer walk silent, awestruck in the New York Public Library; it is a place I do research. I look at the paintings in the Metropolitan Museum mostly for the refreshment of my soul, but sometimes to write about them. And some days, when I am on the East Side and I want a place to write for an hour or so, I sit at the tables in the European sculpture wing, turn my back on a Rodin, sip a cappuccino from the coffee bar, and look out the large windows at the park, at dogs, at runners.

I understand that my ease in these buildings, my sense that I belong there, means that I have not cast my lot with the poor who, if they were admitted to these buildings, would not be, as I am, freely welcomed. It is impossible to forget the poor in New York City. It is impossible for me not to know that I don't do enough for them. It is not enough to vote against the mayor who is their enemy. It is not enough regularly to give money to the homeless man on our corner, even to read his novel about his time in Vietnam. It is a feature of the Upper West Side that even the homeless have written novels. I live with the shame that I do not do enough because if I want to write, there is too much for me to do. I need the great buildings, what they provide, what they suggest, for my work. So I no longer allow myself to dwell on what it is that allows them to endure.

When I sit down at the desk where I write, it is more cluttered than I would like, but I will not stop to clear it. It is my time—and there is never enough of it—to write.

What makes me feel that I have the right to live this life I live, and then to write about it?

I am where I want to be, where I have always wanted to be. I might have longed for temporary sojourns in one or another of the great capitals of the world, but this is the place I've always wanted to call home.

When I think of writing about this, the models of literature do not serve me. The images of city life in the books I love are not created by people whom I can think of as being much like me, and they do not describe my life. They are created by people who breathe bad air. The light they see the world through is brown or yellow. They are cold and wet. Their food is disagreeable. The city teaches them their own loathesomeness and the loathesomeness or misfortunes of their neighbors. Often, the writers are contemptuous; they may be envious. Usually, they are men.

Because only men can walk the dark streets by themselves and this, this solitariness lived out in darkness, this
return to a lone room at the top of filthy stairs, this is the
city experience I learned to trust, the one I first believed
in as a reader. How could such a journey be made by a
woman? If the streets are dark and wet and lonely, if there
is the sound in the brown air of a pair of heels on pave-
ment, there is danger lurking. What knowledge is possible
after ravishment? Where can she go from there? She can
go home. Only home. Instead of further exploration: res-
ignation. Or, staying in her room, aging, increasingly
headachy, solitary, first from choice, then from no choice
at all. Her reading glasses will grow stronger every year,
magnifying not only the print of what she reads and her
fine eyes but also the wine-colored pouches below them.
At the approach of a storm (it is always November for this
woman) she pours herself a glass of whiskey; the ice clicks
against the glass. She takes off her high heels.

Of course there were other stories, stories I read
avidly, hungrily even, stories that may have helped propel
me from home, stories of penthouse views (not *Marjorie
Morningstar*, not someplace with parents in residence). The
whoosha-whoosh of cocktail shakers, stories that include
the names Sardi's or Delmonico's or Cartier. But I never
liked the women in these stories; they were superficial,
their happiness was tied to an excessive love of fashion.
They were wives of rich men, or mistresses. Anyway, a
rich man paid the bills.

I am married, I have children, but I am not supported
by a rich man. I am neither old nor lonely, although I

sometimes wonder if I am "no longer young." Oh, I
know that there are others, even in positions of authority,
younger than I. Doctors. Policemen. People who can
refuse me mortgages or life insurance. But does this mean
I am "no longer young"?

How do I speak of all this? How, without incurring
the suspicion that, accompanying the joyous click of the
tongue in the lock's groove of a beloved New York apartment, is an automatic sense of triumphalism? A smug "I'm
here, therefore you're not." A satisfaction, like the ripple of
an ocean breeze, of possession and exclusion.

I do not feel this; what I feel is gratitude, gratitude
toward an institution, and how do I write that, without
feeling embarrassingly jejune about that? Nevertheless it
is the truth. I am where I am because of the benevolence
of an institution. The same one that admitted me as a student and opened the world to me hired me later to teach
young women like my former self, and provided me with
a dwelling so that I could afford to live in this place. This
here. The here that was always the here for me. The here
that allowed me for the first time to have the same kind of
youth that others of my age were having, so that when I
left I was younger than I was when, four years earlier, I
arrived.

But how can I mark or name the day of my arrival.
How can I say anything except, "Now I am here."